Prayers and Proclamations for the Christian Warrior

Dr. Mike Spaulding

The Transforming Word Publishing
PO Box 3007
Elida, OH 45807

The Transforming Word Publishing is a ministry of the House of Spaulding, an ecclesiastical ministry to the body of Christ worldwide. We serve Yahweh alone.

ISBN: 9798329973198

DEDICATION

This book is dedicated to the believers of Calvary Chapel of Lima. This ecclesia has been a constant source of support and encouragement to my wife Kathy and me. We love you all and appreciate your unwavering friendship and trust.

ACKNOWLEDGMENTS

This book is the product of the Holy Spirit. Without question, He impressed upon me several years ago that speaking the Word of God during our ecclesia gatherings in a set aside time that we call “Our Proclamation” was a necessary and powerful reminder that God declares His Word to be true and faithful. Thank you, Father, for guiding us through every season of ministry common to man. We are holding on tight and believing in Your path for us.

INTRODUCTION

Literature is a powerful influence. English author Edward Bulwer-Lytton is credited with first penning the phrase, "The pen is mightier than the sword." Indeed, it is. Literature inspires and captivates. It is able to motivate, encourage, inform, and correct. Literature in the hands of a skilled orator can move people to action. It is able to admonish and rebuke in the same narrative. Literature is often a two-edged sword, which cuts to the quick, revealing hidden agendas and meanings.

The Bible has been studied through the centuries as a great work of literature. I remember many years ago taking a course in the Bible as literature. Of course, no discussions were permitted that went beyond cursory.

Today, Bible believing Christians spend a great amount of time studying the Bible to understand the meaning of it both contextually and exegetically.

As a Bible teacher and pastor, I find it important to

understand what the Bible said and how it was interpreted by the original recipients. That is the starting point for any teaching.

What I have found over the years is the Bible speaks to us today unlike any other book ever written. In its pages are priceless instructions, foundational faith principles, applications and implications for how to live out a true biblical faith.

One of many subjects worth exploring today is the authority granted to each believer in Christ. There have been many books written on this subject in the previous twenty years. Some of these books are accurate in their understanding and some of them are little more than conjecture, stretching credibility to fit into a preconceived understanding that frankly, is not supported by the Bible itself.

This book focuses on one aspect of the authority of every born-again believer in the Lord Jesus Christ. Did you know that every son and daughter of God has authority? You may come from a tradition that does not teach on the believer's authority so, this concept is foreign to you. In order to describe what I am talking about ask yourself the following question. What is a prayer and proclamation and how does it demonstrate authority? Are you able to answer that question? If you were able, how did you respond? Let's discuss this further.

A proclamation is something spoken verbally. It is from a

word that means to "shout forth." In the Hebrew, it means to both speak and hear. Additionally, the word means to hear or listen attentively and obey.[1]

This is the intention behind David's words in **Psalm 26:7** where he says, "That I may proclaim with the voice of thanksgiving and declare all Your wonders." This verse carries the idea of speaking with authority concerning the things of God; doing so with conviction and assertiveness and exhorting all who hear to obey the Word of God.

In the New Testament, the word proclaim is associated closely with preaching the Gospel. **Mark 1:45** for example, says, "But he went out and began to proclaim it freely and to spread the news around, to such an extent that Jesus could no longer publicly enter a city, but stayed out in unpopulated areas; and they were coming to Him from everywhere." The Greek word for proclaim in this verse is *kerysso* and means to proclaim, announce, preach publicly and with conviction or authority.[2]

I am laying this foundation for understanding what it means for a believer in the Lord Jesus Christ to proclaim His Word with authority because like many other things in our world today, the purpose and meaning of proclaiming has been hijacked and misused within the church. This unfortunate situation has led to many Christian's turning away from such things, believing

---

[1] See Strong's Hebrew 8085.
[2] See Strong's 2784.

them to be heresy.

In this context I'm speaking specifically about adherents of the so-called New Apostolic Reformation (NAR) and others who advance a Word Faith theology. Some believe that reality is changed or created according to what is proclaimed, declared, and, or, believed. This is not what I am advocating, nor do I believe that thinking is biblical.

However, I do see numerous examples of believers speaking the Word of God to others with power, conviction, and in the authority that they have by the Holy Spirit with amazing results.

Jesus Himself taught the disciples to proclaim with power His words. **Matthew 10:24-27** says,

> **24** "A disciple is not above his teacher, nor a slave
> above his master. **25** It is enough for the disciple
> that he become like his teacher, and the slave like
> his master. If they have called the head of the
> house Beelzebul, how much more *will they
> malign* the members of his household!
>
> **26** "Therefore do not fear them, for there is nothing
> concealed that will not be revealed, or hidden that
> will not be known. **27** What I tell you in the
> darkness, speak in the light; and what you
> hear *whispered* in *your* ear, proclaim upon the
> housetops.

Joshua 1:8-9

8 This book of the law shall not depart from your mouth,
but you shall meditate on it day and night, so that you
may be careful to do according to all that is written in
it; for then you will make your way prosperous, and then
you will have success. 9 Have I not commanded you? Be
strong and courageous! Do not tremble or be dismayed,
for the LORD your God is with you wherever you go."

Our Proclamation From Joshua 1:8-9

Your Word, Father, will always be in my mouth and on my lips. I will speak it and meditate upon it day and night so that it will guide my every thought, word, and deed according to all You have spoken. As I in humble obedience align my life with You and Your Word, then You will make my way prosperous and successful as You define those things. You have commanded me to be strong and courageous and so I will be strong and courageous. You have told me not to tremble or be dismayed and therefore, I will not tremble or be dismayed, because You have promised to go with me wherever I go.

Galatians 3:13-14

[13] Christ redeemed us from the curse of the Law, having become a curse for us—for it is written, "CURSED IS EVERYONE WHO HANGS ON A TREE"— [14] in order that in Christ Jesus the blessing of Abraham might come to the Gentiles, so that we would receive the promise of the Spirit through faith.

Our Proclamation From Galatians 3:13-14

Christ redeemed me from the curse of the Law, which was death (the wages of sin is death – Romans 6:23a). Jesus did that by deliberately and willing doing the Father's will, submitting Himself to ridicule, abuse, torture, and death on the Cross. In that very act of obedience to the Father Jesus made the way of salvation available to all people, fulfilling God's promise to Abraham that from his lineage, the whole world would be blessed. As a reminder of the fulfillment of God's promise to Abraham and of its fulfillment in Christ, we have been given the Holy Spirit, who lives within us.

Romans 8:1-4

1 Therefore there is now no condemnation for those who
are in Christ Jesus. 2 For the law of the Spirit of
life in Christ Jesus has set you free from the law of sin
and of death. 3 For what the Law could not do, weak as it
was through the flesh, God *did*: sending His own Son
in the likeness of sinful flesh and *as an offering* for sin,
He condemned sin in the flesh, 4 so that the requirement
of the Law might be fulfilled in us, who do not walk
according to the flesh but according to the Spirit.

Our Proclamation From Romans 8:1-4

Because I am now in Christ Jesus by faith, I am no longer under condemnation. Any condemnation spoken to or about me is not from God but from the devil. Christ's death released me from the law of sin and of death and set me free through faith. The abiding and indwelling Holy Spirit is testimony to this truth. It is only by faith that I am born-again and thus in Christ Jesus free from the power of sin. The Law could not do that for me, that is, free me from sin because of the weakness of my own flesh. But Jesus did what I could not do, by submitting Himself as the Father's offering for my sin. Thus, Christ Jesus fulfilled the requirement of the Law for me. All glory and praise to God!

Philippians 4:10-13

10 But I rejoiced in the Lord greatly, that now at last you
have revived your concern for me; indeed, you were
concerned *before*, but you lacked opportunity. 11 Not that
I speak from want, for I have learned to be content in
whatever circumstances I am. 12 I know how to get along
with humble means, and I also know how to live in
prosperity; in any and every circumstance I have learned
the secret of being filled and going hungry, both of
having abundance and suffering need. 13 I can do all
things through Him who strengthens me.

Our Proclamation From Philippians 4:10-13

I rejoice in the Lord greatly when He moves upon the minds and hearts of others to support me in prayer, friendship, or finances. When I mention finances, some people will think I am in need. But that is not necessarily the case. I have learned to be content in whatever circumstances I find myself in. Indeed, I have learned to get along with few or no worldly possessions of value and I have learned to get along when I have an abundance of worldly possessions of value. In whatever circumstance I find myself in I have learned the secret that determines my perspective and heart whether I am in need or in abundance. That secret is this – I can do whatever Christ calls me to do in spite of my circumstances; whether I have abundance when He calls, or I have little when He calls. His call comes with His provision of strength to endure and succeed in the call.

Romans 10-9-11

9 that if you confess with your mouth Jesus *as* Lord,
and believe in your heart that God raised Him from the
dead, you will be saved; 10 for with the heart a person
believes, resulting in righteousness, and with the mouth
he confesses, resulting in salvation. 11 For the Scripture
says, "WHOEVER BELIEVES IN HIM WILL NOT
BE DISAPPOINTED."

Our Proclamation From Romans 10:9-11

I have confessed verbally that Jesus is my Lord. I have believed in my heart (the seat of my emotional and intellectually understanding), that Yahweh raised Yeshua from the dead. Believing these things were done on my behalf, I am born-again (saved). With my mind/intellect I believe in the name of Yeshua, and the result of my faith is the receiving of the righteousness of Yeshua. The result of my verbal confession of faith is my salvation. Therefore, on the day when Yeshua returns or I leave this life behind in death, I will not be disappointed, meaning found to fall short of the glory of Yahweh, because Yeshua is my salvation.

Ephesians 1:3-8a

3 Blessed *be* the God and Father of our Lord Jesus Christ,
who has blessed us with every spiritual blessing in the
heavenly *places* in Christ, 4 just as He chose us in Him
before the foundation of the world, that we would be holy
and blameless before Him. In love 5 He predestined us
to adoption as sons through Jesus Christ to
Himself, according to the kind intention of His will, 6 to
the praise of the glory of His grace, which He freely
bestowed on us in the Beloved. 7 In Him we
have redemption through His blood, the forgiveness of
our trespasses, according to the riches of His
grace 8 which He lavished on us.

Our Proclamation From Ephesians 1:3-8

I bless my Father in heaven and my Savior and Lord Jesus Christ for the spiritual blessings my Father has given to me in Jesus, among them salvation and my eternal life and inheritance. I bless my heavenly Father because He chose me and called me before He created the universe. I bless my Father in heaven because His plan, purpose, and provision for me are to live a holy and blameless life before Him. He has declared His intent for me as an adopted son/daughter because of His kindness toward me and the insurmountable grace He bestowed on me in Jesus. He has redeemed me by the blood of Jesus. He has forgiven me all my trespasses because of His magnificent grace which He lavishes on me day by day.

Psalm 17:3-5

3 You have tried my heart, you have visited me by night,
you have tested me, and you will find nothing; I have
purposed that my mouth will not transgress. 4 With regard
to the works of man, by the word of your lips I have
avoided the ways of the violent. 5 My steps have held fast
to your paths; my feet have not slipped.

Our Proclamation From Psalm 17:3-5

Father, You have looked deeply into my inner being. You have spoken to me about the things You have found. You have visited me even in the stillness of the night. Testing and trying me, You have found me to be yielded to You and desiring that You find nothing of which I must repent, because I have proposed in my heart that my mouth will not transgress against You. In my actions, I will not join those who commit violence. Instead, my steps will hold fast to Your paths, and You will cause me to not stubble or fall.

All of God's people say, Amen!

Colossians 1:9-14

9 For this reason, since the day we heard about you, we have not stopped praying for you. We continually ask God to fill you with the knowledge of his will through all the wisdom and understanding that the Spirit gives, 10 so that you may live a life worthy of the Lord and please him in every way: bearing fruit in every good work, growing in the knowledge of God, 11 being strengthened with all power according to his glorious might so that you may have great endurance and patience, 12 and giving joyful thanks to the Father, who has qualified you to share in the inheritance of his holy people in the kingdom of light. 13 For he has rescued us from the dominion of darkness and brought us into the kingdom of the Son he loves, 14 in whom we have redemption, the forgiveness of sins.

Our Proclamation From Colossians 1:9-14

I continually pray that my heavenly Father will fill me with the knowledge of His will, with His wisdom, and with understanding that the Holy Spirit gives. With these things I am able to live a life worthy of the Lord, pleasing Him in every way: (1) bearing fruit in good works, (2) growing in my knowledge of God, (3) being strengthened with/by His power that I might (3) obtain and demonstrate great endurance and patience. I will joyfully give my heavenly Father thanksgiving because He has caused me to be born again into His kingdom of light, rescuing me from the power of the kingdom of darkness. This the Father accomplished by redeeming us through the shed blood of Jesus, which results in the forgiveness of sins through faith.

2 Corinthians 9:10-15

[10] Now He who supplies seed to the sower and bread for
food will supply and multiply your seed for sowing
and increase the harvest of your righteousness; [11] you will
be enriched in everything for all liberality, which through
us is producing thanksgiving to God. [12] For the ministry
of this service is not only fully supplying the needs of
the saints but is also overflowing through many
thanksgivings to God. [13] Because of the proof given by
this ministry, they will glorify God for *your* obedience to
your confession of the gospel of Christ and for the
liberality of your contribution to them and to all, [14] while
they also, by prayer on your behalf, yearn for you
because of the surpassing grace of God in you. [15] Thanks
be to God for His indescribable gift!

Our Proclamation From 2 Corinthians 9:10-15

God is the One who supplies "seed" in my life and provision to multiple my seed that results in an abundant harvest of righteousness in me. I am being enriched in everything so that I may liberally sow into others, all to the praise, glory, and thanksgiving to my God. This ministry which God has raised me up for is supplying the needs of the saints resulting in much thanksgiving to God. This sign and seal upon me and the ministry of liberality He has given me, results is the giving of praise to God as others witness my obedience to God's call, and consistent faithfulness to the Gospel of Jesus Christ. Because of God's work in me others pray for me and marvel at the surpassing grace of God in me. I give God all thanks for His indescribable gift!

Proverbs 9:9-11

9 Give *instruction* to a wise man and he will be still wiser,
Teach a righteous man and he will increase *his* learning.
10 The fear of the LORD is the beginning of wisdom,
And the knowledge of the Holy One is understanding.
11 For by me your days will be multiplied,
And years of life will be added to you.

Our Proclamation From Proverbs 9:9-11

I am a wise man/woman because I have received instruction from the Lord. I desire to always have a teachable spirit so that I will increase in learning and righteousness. I fear the Lord, and I am in awe of His holiness. This is the beginning and foundation of the wisdom He has granted to me. As I grow in learning and understanding my days become full of the favor, provision, and abundance of the Lord in my spirit and soul. My life becomes impactful for His glory, and I become a vessel that honors Him in all I do.

2 Chronicles 14:11-12

11 Then Asa called to the LORD his God and said, "LORD,
there is no one besides You to help *in the battle* between
the powerful and those who have no strength; so help us,
O LORD our God, for we trust in You, and in Your name
have come against this multitude. O LORD, You are our
God; let not man prevail against
You." 12 So the LORD routed the Ethiopians before Asa
and before Judah, and the Ethiopians fled.

Our Proclamation From 2 Chronicles 14:11-12

I will call on the LORD my God. My testimony is that "There is none like You. There is none like You to help me in my battles against those who are powerful. I have no strength of my own to defeat this enemy, so help me O LORD my God. I trust in You, and I stand against every enemy in Your name. My LORD do not let your enemies prevail against you. I will stand firm and witness my God's defeat of His enemies.

Psalm 27:1-3

1 The LORD is my light and my salvation;
Whom shall I fear?
The LORD is the defense of my life;
Whom shall I dread?
2 When evildoers came upon me to devour my flesh,
My adversaries and my enemies, they stumbled and fell.
3 Though a host encamp against me,
My heart will not fear;
Though war arise against me,
In *spite of* this I shall be confident.

Our Proclamation From Psalm 27:1-3

Because Yahweh is my light and salvation, I have no reason to allow fear to grip me and cause me to turn away from trusting Him. Yahweh is my defense; He is my protection and has my life in His hands. There is no need for me to be apprehensive or tremble. When wicked and evil people stand against me in order to do me harm, Yahweh will provide for me in that moment. Those who come against me will ultimately fail to achieve their evil desires because Yahweh will judge all evil. In spite of the numbers, whether a whole host come against me, I will not fear because my confidence is in Yahweh to deliver me from this present travail.

Psalm 27:4-6

[4] One thing I ask from the LORD, this only do I seek: that
I may dwell in the house of the LORD all the days of my
life, to gaze on the beauty of the LORD
and to seek him in his temple. [5] For in the day of trouble
he will keep me safe in his dwelling; he will hide me in
the shelter of his sacred tent and set me high upon a rock.
[6] Then my head will be exalted above the enemies who
surround me; at his sacred tent I will sacrifice with shouts
of joy; I will sing and make music to the LORD.

Our Proclamation From Psalm 27:4-6

There is one thing that occupies my thoughts more than any other; one thing that I desire above all other things. That one thing is to abide in the presence of the LORD all the days of my life. I desire above all other things to behold the beauty of the LORD and to seek Him in worship, praising Him and honoring Him with my life (in His temple). When trouble comes to me, He will keep me safely abiding in His presence, and make my footing secure upon the rock that is Jesus Christ. Then, as I behold His beauty during my trouble, safe and secure from debilitating troubles of this life, He will lift my countenance (my head) above my enemies (fear, despair, depression, additions, bondages, etc.). Therefore, I will offer to Him my sacrifices of praise, the fruit of my lips

(Hebrews 13:15), which is sweet music to the ears of Yahweh.

Psalm 27:7-10

7 Hear, O LORD, when I cry with my voice,
And be gracious to me and answer me.
8 *When You said*, "Seek My face," my heart said to You,
"Your face, O LORD, I shall seek."
9 Do not hide Your face from me,
Do not turn Your servant away in anger;
You have been my help;
Do not abandon me nor forsake me,
O God of my salvation!
10 For my father and my mother have forsaken me,
But the LORD will take me up.

Our Proclamation From Psalm 27:7-10

Thank you for hearing my cry, O LORD. Thank you for your gracious answer to my plea. You have instructed me to seek Your face, and my heart responds to Your call that "I shall seek Your face." I am thankful that You do not hide Your face from me and that You do not turn away from me in Your anger. You have always been my help; You have never abandoned nor forsook me. You are my salvation! People may forsake me, but You never will.

1 Thessalonians 5:16-24

16 Rejoice always; 17 pray without ceasing; 18 in
everything give thanks; for this is God's will for you in
Christ Jesus. 19 Do not quench the Spirit; 20 do not
despise prophetic utterances. 21 But examine
everything *carefully*; hold fast to that which is
good; 22 abstain from every form of evil.

23 Now may the God of peace Himself sanctify you
entirely; and may your spirit and soul and body be
preserved complete, without blame at the coming of our
Lord Jesus Christ. 24 Faithful is He who calls you, and He
also will bring it to pass.

Our Proclamation From 1 Thessalonians 5:16-24

Yahweh has given me the ability to be grateful and so that will be my focus. Yahweh has granted me the great privilege to speak with Him and so I will never grow weary of praying. These two things are Yahweh's will for me, and I am able to do both because I am born-again through faith in Jesus. I will not ignore Yahweh's leading because I do not want to quench His Holy Spirit. I will listen with spiritual ears to prophetic voices, examining everything and discarding that which is not of Yahweh. I pray Yahweh's peace and sanctifying work upon my brothers and sisters of the faith, and for their welfare in this life so that they are ready and blameless at the return of our Savior and Lord Jesus Christ. Yahweh is faithful in all that He proclaims and does, and He will bring His will to pass.

Proverbs 3:1-8

1 My son, do not forget my teaching, but let your
heart keep my commandments; 2 For length of days and
years of life and peace they will add to you. 3 Do not
let kindness and truth leave you; Bind them around your
neck, write them on the tablet of your heart. 4 So you
will find favor and good repute in the sight of God and
man. 5 Trust in the LORD with all your heart and do not
lean on your own understanding. 6 In all your ways
acknowledge Him, and He will make your paths straight.
7 Do not be wise in your own eyes; Fear the LORD and
turn away from evil. 8 It will be healing to your body
and refreshment to your bones.

Our Proclamation From Proverbs 3:1-8

My Father, I will not forget Your teaching. Thank you for enabling me to incline my heart to keep Your commandments. You tell me that when I obey Your commandments days and years as well as Your peace will be added to my life. You have instructed me to maintain kindness and truth as my constant companions; that I am to bind them to my neck and heart so that they are ever before me as a reminder of how I am to relate to You and my fellow man. I will trust in You with all my heart and that means I will not trust in my own understanding, but instead will always ask for Your counsel oh God. In everything that I do I will seek Your counsel so that the way that I live will be straight according to the path You desire me to walk and thus not crooked or perverse as the flesh and this world would make it. I will not be haughty or arrogant, because pride is believing myself to be wise when I am not. I fear You LORD because You are holy, righteous, and good, and cannot look upon evil, so I will turn away from it. Living my life for you according to Your Word brings healing and refreshment to me in every way.

Joshua 24:14-15

14 "Now, therefore, fear the LORD and serve Him in
sincerity and truth; and put away the gods which your
fathers served beyond the River and in Egypt, and serve
the LORD. 15 If it is disagreeable in your sight to serve
the LORD, choose for yourselves today whom you will
serve: whether the gods which your fathers served which
were beyond the River, or the gods of the Amorites in
whose land you are living; but as for me and my house,
we will serve the LORD."

Our Proclamation From Joshua 24:14-15

Before I can achieve victory over my enemies and the enemies of Yahweh, I must be sure I fear Him (honor and submit to Him in humbleness), and that I am serving Him sincerely and truthfully, for I have no right to expect Yahweh's blessings upon me or my House if I am unfaithful and rebellious. When I am serving Yahweh honorably, sincerely, and truthfully, I will put away the gods I have fashioned in my life. Every day I must make the conscious choice to serve Yahweh and not the idols so prevalent in America. I will declare today and every day that I will serve the LORD and that I am able to serve the LORD through faith in Yeshua ha Mashiach, Jesus the Christ.

1 John 2:15-17

15 Do not love the world nor the things in the world. If
anyone loves the world, the love of the Father is not in
him. 16 For all that is in the world, the lust of the flesh
and the lust of the eyes and the boastful pride of life, is
not from the Father, but is from the world. 17 The world is
passing away, and *also* its lusts; but the one who does the
will of God lives forever.

Our Proclamation From 1 John 2:15-17

Because my heavenly Father has commanded me to not love the world or all the things of the world, I will not love it or them. I understand that the world means the world system which is antithetical to my Father's design and intent, and the things of the world are all the things that try to allure me away from my Father's mission for me in His world through distraction, deceit, and false promises of contentment. The world and the things of the world fall into three broad categories that my Father calls the lust of the flesh, the lust of the eyes, and the boastful pride of life. The lust of the flesh seeks to incite my natural physical needs to abuse the things Yahweh has called goo. The lust of the eyes seeks to incite me to covetousness, jealousy, or sexual sin. The pride of life seeks to incite me to self-promotion, boastfulness, and arrogance. These things are not from my Father but are earthly and passing away. Instead of allowing these things to control and ruin me, I will seek to do the will of my Father who empowers me by faith in Jesus and the enabling grace of the indwelling Holy Spirit.

Colossians 2:6-10

6 Therefore as you have received Christ Jesus the
Lord, *so* walk in Him, 7 having been firmly rooted *and*
now being built up in Him and established in your faith,
just as you were instructed, *and* overflowing with
gratitude.

8 See to it that no one takes you captive
through philosophy and empty deception, according to
the tradition of men, according to the elementary
principles of the world, rather than according to
Christ. 9 For in Him all the fullness of Deity dwells in
bodily form, 10 and in Him you have
been made complete, and He is the head over all rule and
authority.

Our Proclamation From Colossians 2:6-9

Because I trusted in Jesus for eternal life, I am enabled by the Holy Spirit to walk in Him. That means I have the power of the Holy Spirit in me to obey Yahweh's commandments out of a heart of love for Him. That is what it means to be firmly rooted in Jesus, to be in the process of being built up in my faith. These are things the Word of Yahweh instructs me to do, and I am overflowing with gratitude for His gift of salvation through Jesus.

I also have a responsibility to test all things because in this world there are philosophies of men that are deceptions that if I heed them, will take me captive and lead me away from Christ. These traditions of men will seek my worship. They will attempt to replace my love and devotion for Jesus. Therefore, I will always keep in mind that Jesus is Yahweh's gift to me to rescue me from the snares of the enemy, and I am completed, made whole, and loved by my heavenly Father because I abide in Jesus' loving embrace.

1 John 4:1-6

1 Beloved, do not believe every spirit, but test the spirits
to see whether they are from God, because many false
prophets have gone out into the world. 2 By this you
know the Spirit of God: every spirit that confesses
that Jesus Christ has come in the flesh is from God; 3 and
every spirit that does not confess Jesus is not from God;
this is the *spirit* of the antichrist, of which you have heard
that it is coming, and now it is already in the world. 4 You
are from God, little children, and have overcome them;
because greater is He who is in you than he who is in the
world. 5 They are from the world; therefore they
speak *as* from the world, and the world listens to
them. 6 We are from God; he who knows God listens to
us; he who is not from God does not listen to us. By this
we know the spirit of truth and the spirit of error.

Our Proclamation From 1 John 4:1-6

I am beloved by my Father in heaven. Because His love abides upon me and in me, I have the ability to examine every spirit that animates behavior, words, and actions, and identify those animating spirits that are not from Yahweh. Because Yahweh has given me this gift of discernment, I see animating spirits that are not from Yahweh. Therefore, I will reject the false prophets speaking falsehoods. The Holy Spirit of my Father resides in me and therefore, I see that those who cannot confess that Jesus the Christ, the Son of Yahweh, came into this world as the divine yet human God-man, do not belong to Yahweh through faith in Jesus/Yeshua. Those who deny that Jesus as the Son of Yahweh became man are modern day Gnostics, indeed this animating spirit is alive today and actively deceiving millions of people. I am thankful that I belong to Yahweh and because of Calvary's Cross and Jesus' death, resurrection, and ascension to the right hand of the Father, I have overcome the world and all the wickedness of the world. As a testimony to this victory, I will give witness to the salvation the Father offers through faith in Jesus. Those who will not listen are still under the power of the spirit of this age.

Philippians 2:1-4

1 Therefore if there is any encouragement in Christ, if
there is any consolation of love, if there is any fellowship
of the Spirit, if any affection and compassion, 2 make my
joy complete by being of the same mind, maintaining the
same love, united in spirit, intent on one purpose. 3 Do
nothing from selfishness or empty conceit, but with
humility of mind regard one another as more important
than yourselves; 4 do not *merely* look out for your own
personal interests, but also for the interests of others.

Our Proclamation From Philippians 2:1-4

I am encouraged by Jesus Christ daily; comforted by His love daily; Indwelt by His Holy Spirit. Therefore, I can show affection and compassion for others. These things are enabled by Yahweh's Holy Spirit in me and result in my joy being abundant and complete. Thus, I have the mind of Christ which is common among the brethren as is His love for us all. This brings us into unity and a common purpose in pursuing Christ. I will do nothing from selfish and empty conceit only concerned with myself. Instead, I will demonstrate humility toward my brothers and sisters, regarding them as more important than myself and thus looking out for their personal interests even ahead of my own. This is the unity Jesus prayed we would have as His people.

Matthew 5:1-5

When Jesus saw the crowds, He went up
on the mountain; and after He sat down, His disciples
came to Him. [2] He opened His mouth and *began* to teach
them, saying, [3] "Blessed are the poor in spirit, for theirs is
the kingdom of heaven. [4] "Blessed are those who mourn,
for they shall be comforted. [5] "Blessed are the gentle, for
they shall inherit the earth.

Our Proclamation From Matthew 5:1-5

My Lord and Savior Jesus has taught me where true happiness comes from. When Jesus says I am blessed by being "poor in spirit" He is saying that true, lasting, abiding happiness is available to me when I recognize my complete spiritual destitution apart from Him. Therefore, I will humble myself before Him, recognizing I am not worthy of His blessings, but with a heart of gratitude receive His kindnesses and blessings which accompany my salvation (kingdom of heaven). Because I recognize my spiritual bankruptcy, I mourn and cry out to You oh Lord for the healing balm of Your mercy and forgiveness. Only then am I comforted with true comfort because that comes from You. When I understand who I am before You I am humbled and meek (gentle), considering Your holiness and great love by which You have saved me. Your promise to me is that I will gain eternal life (inherit the earth).

Matthew 5:6-8

6 "Blessed are those who hunger and thirst for
righteousness, for they shall be satisfied.

7 "Blessed are the merciful, for they shall receive mercy.

8 "Blessed are the pure in heart, for they shall see God.

Our Proclamation From Matthew 5:6-8

I find true happiness in Christ when I hunger and thirst for righteousness. Hungering and thirsting means that my motivation is to honor, obey, and glorify Yahweh in all I do. It means that a spiritual life in Christ is lived in the righteousness that He provides. When I am pursuing and experiencing His righteousness, I am truly satisfied.

I find true happiness when I am merciful. Being merciful leaves no room for pride, self-righteousness, or judgmentalism. When I am merciful to people Yahweh is merciful to me.

I find true happiness when I am pure in heart. I am only pure in heart because of the gift of salvation given to me in Christ by faith. Therefore, I fix my gaze upon Christ with single-minded devotion, spiritual integrity, and motivation to holy living.

Matthew 5:9

9 "Blessed are the peacemakers, for they shall be called sons of God.

Our Proclamation From Matthew 5:9

You, Father, are a God of peace. I have great happiness LORD when I understand Your peace. Mankind's peace was stolen by the evil one in Eden, but You Yeshua, brought the hope of peace to a lost world at Bethlehem and restored it at Calvary. Your peace Father is based on Your righteousness which I received by faith in Jesus Christ. Your righteousness that became mine leads me to seek the highest and best for others. Your Word Father instructs me to pursue peace with all men, and the sanctification that results in, without which no one will see You LORD.

You also told me Lord Jesus that You did not come to bring peace, but a sword (Matthew 10:34). This tells me that You are not speaking of peace at any cost. Your peace comes on Your terms. That means truth, righteousness, and holiness are the foundations of Your peace. I should expect the world to offer division, strife, discord, and hatred toward my efforts to bring Your peace. Your peace cannot come where sin remains. This is the ministry of reconciliation by which I and others are known as Your sons and daughters. Therefore, the true

Gospel of Jesus Christ is the only way that Your peace will reign upon the earth. LORD equip me to be Your peacemaker.

Matthew 5:10-12

10 "Blessed are those who have been persecuted for the sake of righteousness, for theirs is the kingdom of heaven.

11 "Blessed are you when *people* insult you and persecute
you, and falsely say all kinds of evil against you because
of Me. 12 Rejoice and be glad, for your reward in heaven
is great; for in the same way they persecuted the prophets
who were before you.

Our Proclamation From Matthew 5:10-12

Father, your Word is perfect and flows exactly as you intend it to. As I have reviewed the first seven of your promised blessings of happiness for those who: (1) are poor in spirit, meaning those who recognize their spiritual emptiness without You; (2) those who mourn, meaning those who are broken over their spiritual condition and turn to You in saving faith; (3) are gentle, because the Holy Spirit lives in us and enables us to manifest the character of Christ; (4) who hunger and thirst for righteousness, meaning that we are motivated to honor, obey, and glorify You in all things; (5) being merciful so that I may receive Your mercy; (6) being pure in heart, meaning I fix my sight upon Christ in devotion, integrity, and holiness; (7) become a peacemaker, meaning I will walk in Your peace which only comes through Your truth, Your righteousness, and Your holiness. Being Your peacemaker means I will commit myself to the ministry of reconciliation on Your terms not the world's terms.

When I clearly understand the happiness that comes from these actions on my part, I must expect to be persecuted. Godly living will receive evil in return. I find my happiness in eternity. Knowing that my reward in heaven is great, I will walk the same path as Your prophets did before me.

1 Peter 5:6-11

6 Therefore humble yourselves under the mighty hand of
God, that He may exalt you at the proper time, 7 casting
all your anxiety on Him, because He cares for you. 8 Be
of sober *spirit*, be on the alert. Your adversary, the devil,
prowls around like a roaring lion, seeking someone to
devour. 9 But resist him, firm in *your* faith, knowing
that the same experiences of suffering are being
accomplished by your brethren who are in the
world. 10 After you have suffered for a little while,
the God of all grace, who called you to His eternal glory
in Christ, will Himself perfect, confirm,
strengthen *and* establish you. 11 To Him *be* dominion
forever and ever. Amen.

Our Proclamation From 1 Peter 5:6-11

I will humble myself under God's mighty hand, so that He will exalt me in His perfect timing. I will cast all my anxious thoughts, all my worry at His feet, because He loves me and cares for me. I will be of sober spirit, on the alert, and watchful, because my adversary, the devil, is constantly hunting his prey like a hungry lion, seeking to devour me. I will resist him, remaining strong and firm in my faith in Jesus, knowing that my brothers and sisters share in my burden and suffering. God will bring me through every trial because He is a God of grace and has given us an eternal home in the glorious presence of

Jesus. Through it all, God will perfect, confirm, strengthen, and establish me in Him. To Jesus Christ belongs all dominion forever and ever.

All of God's people say, Amen!

Psalm 56:1-4

1 Be gracious to me, O God, for man has trampled upon
me; Fighting all day long he oppresses me. 2 My foes
have trampled upon me all day long, for they are many
who fight proudly against me. 3 When I am afraid, I
will put my trust in You. 4 In God, whose word I praise,
In God I have put my trust; I shall not be afraid. What
can *mere* man do to me?

Our Proclamation From Psalm 56:1-4

Father, I need your grace every day in this world, for man tramples upon me constantly. Man is fighting against You in most cases when he/she oppresses me. My enemies seek to silence my witness for You every day. They often do so in their pride, thinking they are right because they have the ability to oppress. When these things come upon me, I turn to You. When fear tries to overcome my knowledge of You, I reject fear and remember to trust in You regardless of the circumstances. When this world comes against me, I refuse to be afraid, remembering that You have said, "What can mere man do to you?"

Isaiah 2:2-4

2 Now it will come about that in the last days
the mountain of the house of the LORD will be
established as the chief of the mountains and will be
raised above the hills; And all the nations will stream to
it. 3 And many peoples will come and say, "Come, let us
go up to the mountain of the LORD, to the house of the
God of Jacob; That He may teach us concerning His
ways and that we may walk in His paths." For the law
will go forth from Zion and the word of the LORD from
Jerusalem. 4 And He will judge between the nations and
will render decisions for many peoples; And they will
hammer their swords into plowshares and their spears
into pruning hooks. Nation will not lift up sword against
nation, and never again will they learn war.

Our Proclamation From Isaiah 2:2-4

Father, I know that this world is in the last days before the return of Jesus for His body. As those days draw near to the end, You are establishing Your house as a sanctuary; a high and holy mountain for all those who love you to seek refuge and peace within. The testimony of the day when You bring Your kingdom upon the earth will be "Come, let us go up to the mountain of the LORD, to the house of the God of Jacob." There we will learn of Your ways and walk in Your paths. In the meantime, Your Word will go out upon the whole earth, and You will render perfect justice and righteous judgment. Your people will turn away from war and all aggression and instead commit themselves to Your peace and Your lovingkindness.

Daniel 3:13-18

13 Then Nebuchadnezzar in furious rage commanded
that Shadrach, Meshach, and Abednego be brought. So
they brought these men before the king.
14 Nebuchadnezzar answered and said to them, “Is it true,
O Shadrach, Meshach, and Abednego, that you do not
serve my gods or worship the golden image that I have
set up? 15 Now if you are ready when you hear the sound
of the horn, pipe, lyre, trigon, harp, bagpipe, and every
kind of music, to fall down and worship the image that I
have made, well and good. But if you do not worship,
you shall immediately be cast into a burning fiery
furnace. And who is the god who will deliver you out of
my hands?”

16 Shadrach, Meshach, and Abednego answered and said
to the king, “O Nebuchadnezzar, we have no need to
answer you in this matter. 17 If this be so, our God whom
we serve is able to deliver us from the burning fiery
furnace, and he will deliver us out of your hand, O
king. 18 But if not, be it known to you, O king, that we
will not serve your gods or worship the golden image that
you have set up.”

Our Proclamation From Daniel 3:13-18

Father, I know that evil people have seized control of the governments of the world. I also know that this was not Your plan, for You decreed that the purpose of government was to be a minister for good as You define good. There is no government on the face of the earth today that serves You. They are all pursuing the course of wickedness and plan to harm and even exterminate those who love You and seek to serve you. Therefore, I declare this day that even though I am threatened, maliciously slandered, and accused of being a subversive enemy of the state, I will not bow my knee to their threats and accept their rebellion against Your authority. I will stand strong in loyal obedience to You, the only true King. I am and will be able to do this by the power of Jesus Christ in me.

Isaiah 9:6-7

6 For a child will be born to us, a son will be given to us;
And the government will rest on His shoulders; And His
name will be called Wonderful Counselor, Mighty God,
Eternal Father, Prince of Peace. 7 There will be no end to
the increase of *His* government or of peace, on the throne
of David and over his kingdom, To establish it and to
uphold it with justice and righteousness from then on and
forevermore. The zeal of the LORD of hosts will
accomplish this.

Our Proclamation From Isaiah 9:6-7

Father, you have fulfilled your promise to Your people Israel and to us, those who have been grafted into the vine, to send Your Son, given for us on Calvary's Cross. You have promised that Your government will rest upon His shoulders. He is known to all who have come to know Him by faith as our Wonderful Counselor. His words are sure, and He will bring to fruition all that He speaks. Therefore, we can trust His counsel. He is our Mighty God, our *el gibbor*, able to do all He has promised. There is none that can stand against Him. He is One with the Father, co-equal, and co-eternal, and our Prince of Peace. He brings an end to the enmity against God through our confession of faith, and the peace that comes through being reconciled with the Father. When He comes, it will mark the beginning of endless peace and the all-consuming government of His righteousness. He is the fulfillment of the promises Yahweh made to David and to the promulgation of his throne in His justice and by His righteousness. The zeal of our great God and Father will accomplish this.

Joshua 14:7-9

7 I was forty years old when Moses the servant of
the LORD sent me from Kadesh-barnea to spy out the
land, and I brought word back to him as *it was* in my
heart. 8 Nevertheless my brethren who went up with me
made the heart of the people melt with fear; but I
followed the LORD my God fully. 9 So Moses swore on
that day, saying, 'Surely the land on which your foot has
trodden will be an inheritance to you and to your children
forever, because you have followed the LORD my God
fully.'

Our Proclamation From Joshua 14:7-9

I may be given an assignment at any or every age of life. Yahweh will give me specific instructions in my assignments. The things that I see that might alarm me in this assignment are not to be considered as too great a thing for Yahweh. In this, He is developing in me, trust in Him. Because my heart is attuned to Him, I can bring back a good report of the things I see in my assignment. Other people may have the same assignment and yet, they show seeds of fear in the lives of others because their heart was not trusting in the LORD. I will follow the LORD fully and not allow my heart to waver. In this believing loyalty to Yahweh, His promises become my inheritance.

1 Corinthians 2:12-13

12 Now we have received, not the spirit of the world, but
the Spirit who is from God, so that we may know the
things freely given to us by God, 13 which things we also
speak, not in words taught by human wisdom, but in
those taught by the Spirit, combining
spiritual *thoughts* with spiritual *words*.

Our Proclamation From 1 Corinthians 2:12-13

Father, I am grateful that I have been freed from the spirit of this world, having received Your Spirit. Your Spirit enables me to know the things You desire that I know. You give Your wisdom to me freely, and to all who reject the world's wisdom and seek Your wisdom. The things I receive from You are the things I freely speak. I do not speak the world's thoughts or wisdom, but the Spirit's thoughts and words spoken to me.

Jude 17-23

[17] But you, beloved, ought to remember the words that
were spoken beforehand by the apostles of our Lord
Jesus Christ, [18] that they were saying to you, "In the last
time there will be mockers, following after their own
ungodly lusts." [19] These are the ones who cause
divisions, worldly-minded, devoid of the Spirit. [20] But
you, beloved, building yourselves up on your most
holy faith, praying in the Holy Spirit, [21] keep yourselves
in the love of God, waiting anxiously for the mercy of
our Lord Jesus Christ to eternal life. [22] And have mercy
on some, who are doubting; [23] save others, snatching
them out of the fire; and on some have mercy with
fear, hating even the garment polluted by the flesh.

Our Proclamation From Jude 17-23

Father, thank you for helping me to keep in mind all the words of the Scriptures which tell me about the spiritual and physical conditions of the last days; that there will mockers of the faith in Your ecclesias and even some who follow their ungodly lusts and testify that they belong to Jesus. These same people cause divisions because of their worldly-mindedness. They do not have Your Holy Spirit. Father help me to continue to grow in my faith, praying in the Spirit and by the Spirit that I will always remain in Your love, eagerly awaiting the return of Jesus and my own rapture from this earth into eternal life. Help me to have mercy on those who struggle, to faithfully proclaim the true Gospel to those who do not believe and are caught up in carnal and fleshly lives.

Psalm 73:21-24

[21] When my heart was embittered
And I was pierced within,
[22] Then I was senseless and ignorant;
I was *like* a beast before You.
[23] Nevertheless I am continually with You;
You have taken hold of my right hand.
[24] With Your counsel You will guide me,
And afterward receive me to glory.

Our Proclamation From Psalm 73:21-24

Father, the devil constantly attempts to deceive me into allowing bitterness to rule my soul. The evil one tries to convince me that I am justified in seeking vengeance, or holding on to animosity, or allowing ungodly thoughts toward others to rule my mind. When I allow the devil to have free reign in my mind, I become bitter and that bitterness is like a piercing arrow that in the end, wounds and even kill me. I become senseless and ignorant which means I cannot hear Your Holy Spirit when he provides the necessary counsel and corrective to free me from this self-induced bondage of my soul. In spite of these schemes of the devil against me, You never leave me and therefore I am continually with You just as if You are holding my right hand. With this glorious truth, I am able to overcome the devil, hear Your counsel that always guides me to truth and freedom of the soul. My future is insured in You and You will receive me into Your glory.

2 Corinthians 2:14-17

14 But thanks be to God, who always leads us in triumph
in Christ, and manifests through us the sweet aroma of
the knowledge of Him in every place. 15 For we are
a fragrance of Christ to God among those who are being
saved and among those who are perishing; 16 to the one
an aroma from death to death, to the other an aroma from
life to life. And who is adequate for these things? 17 For
we are not like many, peddling the word of God, but as
from sincerity, but as from God, we speak in Christ in the
sight of God.

Our Proclamation From 2 Corinthians 2:14-17

All thanksgiving belongs to you Father because you are victorious in all things. You have triumphed over the divine rebels and all wickedness and evil and You lead me by faith into this same victory. Being Your son/daughter means that I exude the sweet aroma of Your grace and mercy found in Jesus Christ wherever I am. Whether among the unbelieving or the believing, my testimony of Your kind and merciful gift of salvation in Jesus is a fragrant offering to You. To those who believe it is a soothing reminder of eternal life to come. For those who disbelieve it is a reminder that You are their Creator, and You desire to show them mercy. I am not adequate for this ministry without You. I recognize that I are not a "merchant" of Your Gospel, attempting to "sell" people on Your mercy, but my testimony is about Jesus and His life-giving gift of salvation, spoken in Your presence for Your glory and honor.

Proverbs 20:1-4

1 Wine is a mocker, strong drink a brawler,
And whoever is intoxicated by it is not wise.
2 The terror of a king is like the growling of a lion;
He who provokes him to anger forfeits his own life.
3 Keeping away from strife is an honor for a man,
But any fool will quarrel.
4 The sluggard does not plow after the autumn,
So he begs during the harvest and has nothing.

Our Proclamation From Proverbs 20:1-4

Father, Your Word is life (John 1:1-4, 14). You give me insight and wisdom when I ask it of You (James 1:5). When I do not ask it of You and seek to live my life without Your presence I stumble into all types of misfortunes (Psalm 14:2-5). Partaking of alcohol with no discipline will lead to its mastery over me. It becomes my mocker and creates within me an attitude of discontent, murmuring, trouble, and uproar (Strongs #1993e – brawler). This behavior is just as foolish as intentionally provoking to anger authorities who rule by terror and not by Your commandments. I am wise when I avoid these types of actions and behaviors. I must steadfastly plow the ministry fields You have blessed me with, not giving in to the path of pleasure or laziness which will bring about my demise in a day of want.

Galatians 5:24-25

24 Now those who belong to Christ Jesus have crucified the flesh with its passions and desires.

25 If we live by the Spirit, let us also walk by the Spirit.

Our Proclamation From Galatians 5:24-25

I belong to Christ by faith in His name (John 3:16; 11:25). When I trust in Jesus for my salvation, I am trusting in His finished work on the cross and His bodily resurrection, ascension, and glorification as the Risen and Exalted Christ. Baptism pictures this total reconstitution of my spirit and soul, in effect my own fleshly nature was crucified with Christ the moment I believed. That means that all thoughts and desires that do not line up with who Jesus is and what being a believer in Jesus looks like biblically, must die, sometimes more than once. Because I know live by the power and leading of the Holy Spirit who lives in me (John 14:17), I can have victory over everything that opposes me because of Christ. Therefore, I will not be boastful about what Yahweh has done in me by challenging others to live up to my standards, nor will I be envious of what Yahweh has done in the lives of others (the context for this passage is the deeds of the flesh versus the fruits of the Spirit).

Isaiah 54:17

No weapon that is formed against you will prosper;
And every tongue that accuses you in judgment you will condemn. This is the heritage of the servants of the LORD, and their vindication is from Me," declares the LORD.

Our Proclamation From Isaiah 54:17

No weapon that is formed against me will prosper. Every tongue that slanders me or gossips about me will be judged and condemned by you Father.

This is my birthright and promise as your son/daughter and servant, Oh God.

My vindication will come from You Father.

Matthew 9:11-13

9 As Jesus went on from there, He saw a man
called Matthew, sitting in the tax collector's booth; and
He said to him, "Follow Me!" And he got up and
followed Him. 10 Then it happened that as Jesus was
reclining *at the table* in the house, behold, many tax
collectors and sinners came and were dining with Jesus
and His disciples. 11 When the Pharisees saw *this*, they
said to His disciples, "Why is your Teacher eating with
the tax collectors and sinners?" 12 But when Jesus
heard *this*, He said, "*It is* not those who are healthy who
need a physician, but those who are sick. 13 But go and
learn what this means: 'I DESIRE COMPASSION, AND NOT
SACRIFICE,' for I did not come to call the righteous, but
sinners."

Our Proclamation From Matthew 9:11-13

Jesus, you demonstrated repeatedly that You see what I often fail to see. You call people to follow You who have some of the most "checkered" pasts. Matthew was a most despised man and yet, he found in You hope, promise, and eternal life, the three things nearly every man or woman seeks. The evidence of Matthew's joy is seen in his invitation to You to join him at his home for a party in which You would meet and speak with his tax collector friends. Religious people do not understand how people unlike them can receive the kindness, mercy, and forgiveness that You freely offer too all. Religious people do not understand that their actions of rejecting those in need of forgiveness means they likely haven't experienced it at all and are still dead in their sins. Thank you, Jesus, for helping me understand that I need Your healing (forgiveness) and that You desire I show others how they can receive the same forgiveness. Thank you for creating in me a heart of compassion for the lost.

Psalm 15:1-3

[1] O LORD, who may abide in Your tent?
Who may dwell on Your holy hill?
[2] He who walks with integrity, and works righteousness,
And speaks truth in his heart.
[3] He does not slander with his tongue,
Nor does evil to his neighbor,
Nor takes up a reproach against his friend.

Our Proclamation From Psalm 15:1-3

LORD, how may I stand in Your tent? How may I abide in Your presence? How may I dwell on Your holy hill? You have taught me O LORD to humble myself before You and to do justice and to love kindness. These things are manifested when I live with integrity and as a righteous servant unto You. Then I am able to hear Your truth spoken to my heart. Integrity and righteousness will not permit me to slander anyone, nor to speak evil of my neighbor, nor to bring an unfounded accusation against my friend.

1 Chronicles 28:20

20 Then David said to his son Solomon, "Be strong and courageous, and act; do not fear nor be dismayed, for the LORD God, my God, is with you. He will not fail you nor forsake you until all the work for the service of the house of the LORD is finished.

Our Proclamation From 1 Chronicles 28:20

King David spoke words of affirmation and encouragement to his son Solomon because You first spoke the same to King David. I am Your son/daughter, and You speak words of affirmation and encouragement to me. Help me to speak the same words of affirmation and encouragement to my spouse, my children, and my family. You encourage me to be strong and courageous throughout Your Word (Deut. 31:6; Joshua 1:7; 2 Samuel 10:12; 1 Chronicles 19:13), and then to act in ways that bring You honor. When I am strong and courageous, I am careful to observe and obey all that Your Word tells me. You have reminded me that You will never leave nor forsake me. Then I am blessed with Your gifts of increased victory and success in the tasks You have set before me.

Matthew 6:7-10

7 "And when you are praying, do not use meaningless
repetition as the Gentiles do, for they suppose that they
will be heard for their many words. 8 So do not be like
them; for your Father knows what you need before you
ask Him.

9 "Pray, then, in this way:

'Our Father who is in heaven,
Hallowed be Your name.
10 'Your kingdom come.
Your will be done,
On earth as it is in heaven.

Our Proclamation From Matthew 6:7-10

Father, I understand from Your instructions about prayer which Jesus shared with us that I am not to use meaningless words or repetition because You are not flattered or impressed by such things. You already know what my needs are before I come to you in prayer. I understand that when I come to Your throne of grace I will acknowledge You as the King and Creator who resides in the third heaven. I will honor Your name in word and deed. I will ask that Your kingdom comes to be established on the earth. I will ask that Your will be done on the earth as it is done in heaven. These things will require me to seek You in all things and in all ways, and to not lean on my own understanding.

Deuteronomy 7:9

Know therefore that the LORD your God, He is God, the faithful God, who keeps His covenant and His lovingkindness to a thousandth generation with those who love Him and keep His commandments.

Our Proclamation From Deuteronomy 7:9

I am a witness to the truth that You are Yahweh, my faithful Father. I testify that You have kept Your covenant of lovingkindness toward me. I testify that I have seen Your faithfulness toward me and my children and my grandchildren as we seek You, serve You, obey You, and love You. Your promise to love us to the thousandth generation will be fulfilled should you tarry, for all those which love You.

Psalm 26:1-7

1 Vindicate me, O LORD, for I have walked in my
integrity, and I have trusted in the LORD without
wavering. 2 Examine me, O LORD, and try me; Test
my mind and my heart. 3 For Your lovingkindness is
before my eyes, and I have walked in Your truth. 4 I do
not sit with deceitful men, nor will I go with pretenders.
5 I hate the assembly of evildoers, and I will not sit with
the wicked. 6 I shall wash my hands in innocence, and I
will go about Your altar, O LORD, 7 That I may proclaim
with the voice of thanksgiving and declare all
Your wonders.

Our Proclamation From Psalm 26:1-7

You have and will continue to vindicate me my God because I have been faithful to You in all my ways and have trusted in You for Your vindication of me. Please continue to examine me, try me, and test my mind and heart, so that I will always walk close to You. My eyes are set on You Father, and I see Your continual lovingkindnesses toward me. I will walk in Your truth. I will not make my habitation among deceitful men, and I will not walk with those with pretend faith. I hate the assembly of evildoers, many of whom call themselves Christians. I will not sit with them. I will cleanse myself from all their defilement so that I may serve You at Your altar and proclaim all Your ways and wonders with a voice and heart of thanksgiving.

2 Corinthians 5:7

for we walk by faith, not by sight…

Our Proclamation From 2 Corinthians 5:7

Father, thank you for the gift of faith. Thank you for the spiritual vision to see things that are not as they will be one day. You saw me in my sin and despair before I had any understanding of You or Your goodness and mercy. Yet, in seeing me, You saw what I could be through faith in Jesus. Faith enables me to move forward against the opposition of this world and its ruler. Faith reminds me that I must not count the things I see as the final answer to anything. This world cannot provide any abiding hope to a son or daughter of Yours. I understand that the things my eyes behold may disappear tomorrow. Only those things done in faith for You will remain.

Ephesians 2:11-13

11 Therefore remember that formerly you, the Gentiles in
the flesh, who are called "Uncircumcision" by the so-
called "Circumcision," *which is* performed in the flesh by
human hands— 12 *remember* that you were at that time
separate from Christ, excluded from the commonwealth
of Israel, and strangers to the covenants of promise,
having no hope and without God in the world. 13 But now
in Christ Jesus you who formerly were far off have been
brought near by the blood of Christ.

Our Proclamation From Ephesians 2:11-13

Father, You have instructed me through Your servant Paul to remember that as a Gentile in the flesh, I was at one time separated from You which meant, separated from You because I had not trusted in Jesus Christ, (Yeshua ha Mashiach) for the salvation of my soul. The Messiah is a distinctly Jewish person and trust. Being separated from You meant I was also not part of the vine that is Israel, which You call the "Commonwealth of Israel." In other words, I was not a part of the family of Your people, God's people, because I was a stranger to Your covenants and Your promises. But now, You have given me hope because You have brought me into Your forever family through the shed blood of Jesus.

Ephesians 2:14-18

14 For He Himself is our peace, who made both *groups*
into one and broke down the barrier of the dividing
wall, 15 by abolishing in His flesh the enmity, *which is* the
Law of commandments *contained* in ordinances, so that
in Himself He might make the two into one new
man, *thus* establishing peace, 16 and might reconcile them
both in one body to God through the cross, by it
having put to death the enmity. 17 AND HE CAME AND
PREACHED PEACE TO YOU WHO WERE FAR AWAY, AND
PEACE TO THOSE WHO WERE NEAR; 18 for through Him we
both have our access in one Spirit to the Father.

Our Proclamation From Ephesians 2:14-18

Father, You have ordained that through Jesus Christ, His sacrifice on the cross and His resurrection unto the glory He had before His incarnation, that I, through faith in Jesus Christ, now have obtained Your peace. This peace that You have given to me, has brought me into the same family as Your people Israel, so that we are now one. You have pictured that for me by breaking down the dividing wall; what was once called the court of the Gentiles in Your temple, that kept Gentiles separated from You. You have abolished in and by the flesh of Jesus, that is to say by His sacrifice, the enmity that existed between Jew and Gentile contained in the ceremonial law (ordinances – feasts sacrifices, offerings, laws of cleanliness, purification, and all outward commandments), so that You could make of the two one new *man*, thereby establishing and making available Your peace for all people. This is what the death of Jesus on The Cross obtained and made available. This peace was given to Gentiles (YOU WHO WERE FAR AWAY) and Jews (THOSE WHO WERE NEAR), giving to both as the one new body the Holy Spirit.

Ephesians 2:18-22

18 for through Him we both have our access in one Spirit
to the Father. 19 So then you are no longer strangers and
aliens, but you are fellow citizens with the saints, and are
of God's household, 20 having been built on the
foundation of the apostles and prophets, Christ Jesus
Himself being the corner *stone*, 21 in whom the whole
building, being fitted together, is growing into a
holy temple in the Lord, 22 in whom you also are
being built together into a dwelling of God in the Spirit.

Our Proclamation From Ephesians 2:18-22

Father, by Your Spirit, through faith in Jesus (for through Him – Jesus is the doorway), You have brought me (given me access) into Your forever family. I am no longer a stranger or an alien to You or Your family, but I am now a citizen of Your kingdom and household along with all the saints, who have been saved by faith in Jesus Christ (the apostle's and prophet's Gospel proclamation) who is my/our foundation and is in fact the chief cornerstone, in whom the whole building, that is the saints, is being fitted together (perfectly brought together for the use of spiritual gifts in the body) and is growing into a holy temple (the ecclesia).

John 5:5-9

5 A man was there who had been ill for thirty-eight
years. 6 When Jesus saw him lying *there*, and knew that
he had already been a long time *in that condition*, He said
to him, "Do you wish to get well?" 7 The sick man
answered Him, "Sir, I have no man to put me into the
pool when the water is stirred up, but while I am coming,
another steps down before me." 8 Jesus said to him, "Get
up, pick up your pallet and walk." 9 Immediately the man
became well, and picked up his pallet and *began* to walk.

Our Proclamation From John 5:5-9

Jesus, You have taught me to look to You for my help. No matter the circumstance, the length of my trial, or my present state of faith, weak or strong, I am to seek You. When You comc to mc and ask mc if I desire to be made well, to rise above my circumstances, to overcome my trials, regardless of my current state of faith, may my mind, heart, soul, and strength cry out to You for my help for that is what You are. Others may cry that no "man" will help them, and in that they consign themselves to continued difficulties. May I always be quick to testify that You are all I need. When You ask me if I desire for You to move in me and through me for healing, for reconciliation, for things I never dreamed possible, may I always say "Yes" to You. Then I will overcome every obstacle placed before me and walk in the victory You give me.

Psalm 36:7-9

[7] How precious is Your lovingkindness, O God!
And the children of men take refuge in the shadow of
Your wings.
[8] They drink their fill of the abundance of Your house;
And You give them to drink of the river of Your delights.
[9] For with You is the fountain of life;
In Your light we see light.

Our Proclamation From Psalm 36:7-9

Father, Your lovingkindness is precious to me. I am Your son/daughter and I take refuge under Your mighty hand of protection. I drink my fill from the abundance of Your house and from the deep river of Your blessings and favor. You are my fountain of life and my Light that guides my life daily.

Psalm 17:7-8

6 I have called upon You, for You will answer me, O
God;
Incline Your ear to me, hear my speech.
7 Wondrously show Your lovingkindness,
O Savior of those who take refuge at Your right hand
From those who rise up *against them.*
8 Keep me as the apple of the eye;
Hide me in the shadow of Your wings.

Our Proclamation From Psalm 17:7-8

Father, I am encouraged to pray without ceasing in Your Word (1 Thessalonians 5:17). You are faithful in all Your ways, and to those who follow You (Psalm 103:18). You do not withhold any good thing from those who live with integrity before You (Psalm 84:11). This is a truth I hold onto – You will answer my prayers. You will listen to me (incline Your ear). How wonderous is Your lovingkindness toward me. You are my Savior and also to those who take refuge in You. You will be my protector against those who seek to harm me. Just as Your people Israel remain the apple of Your eye, so are all those who trust in Jesus for eternal life.

2 Peter 1:16-18

16 For we did not follow cleverly devised tales when we
made known to you the power and coming of our Lord
Jesus Christ, but we were eyewitnesses of His
majesty. 17 For when He received honor and glory from
God the Father, such an utterance as this was made to
Him by the Majestic Glory, "This is My beloved Son
with whom I am well-pleased"— 18 and we ourselves
heard this utterance made from heaven when we were
with Him on the holy mountain.

Our Proclamation From 2 Peter 1:16-18

Father Your Word tells me that the announcement of the birth of King Jesus and His life lived in obedient love for You, were not fanciful tales based on folklore, myth, or of pagan origin. You established the truthfulness of redemption through faith in my risen Lord by eyewitness accounts which were not then and have not now ever been refuted. We are eyewitnesses of the supernatural and miraculous power attendant upon Jesus for healing, for life, and for the promise of eternal life. You bestowed Your glory and honor upon Jesus on the Mount of Transfiguration and by three eyewitnesses, Peter, James, and John, the brother of James, verified Your prophetic Word through Jesus. Therefore, I am able to stand firm upon who Jesus is and the purpose of His coming to the earth because Your testimony is true.

2 Peter 1:19-21

19 *So* we have the prophetic word *made* more sure, to
which you do well to pay attention as to a lamp shining
in a dark place, until the day dawns and the morning star
arises in your hearts. 20 But know this first of all, that no
prophecy of Scripture is *a matter* of one's own
interpretation, 21 for no prophecy was ever made by an act
of human will, but men moved by the Holy Spirit spoke
from God.

Our Proclamation From 2 Peter 1:19-21

Father, I have Your "prophetic word made more sure," which means that I have Your Word, which is stable and reliable, as if "set in stone," to trust in. Thus, You have given me Your Word which is superior to any experience I might have or to any prophecy another man or woman might give. Jesus told me that "Heaven and earth shall pass away, but My words will never pass away" (Matthew 24:35). I am in no way diminishing the importance of the supernatural encounters I have had with You. Your Word is a lamp shining into the darkness of this world and You tell me to fix my attention (give heed KJV – Greek pros-echo Strongs #4337 – fix my mind firmly upon) Your Word. When I do this, the darkness will be overcome by Your light. When I fix my thoughts and attention upon Your Word, it becomes a great light like the morning star, that floods my soul and I become a light-bearer for You to others. This is why Your Word tells me to not displace Your Word with my own private and self-generated interpretations. I will speak Your Word and teach others as the Holy Spirit moves me. This means I will align my life with You and make every preparation for holy and righteous living so that when Your Holy Spirit moves, I am situated to be moved. This is the only manner in which You have chosen to speak through Your servants in any age.

John 16:8-11

[8] And He, when He comes, will convict the world
regarding sin, and righteousness, and
judgment: [9] regarding sin, because they do not believe in
Me; [10] and regarding righteousness, because I am going
to the Father and you no longer *are going to* see
Me; [11] and regarding judgment, because the ruler of this
world has been judged.

Our Proclamation From John 16:8-11

Jesus, you have told me in Your Word that when the Holy Spirit came, He convicted the world regarding sin, righteousness, and judgment. The Holy Spirit convicts those in unbelief because they are still in their sin. The Holy Spirit thus works in tandem with the Gospel proclamation. The Holy Spirit brings conviction of righteousness because after You ascended Lord Jesus, I am responsible to be Your righteous representative. This is what it means to be an imager of Yahweh. The Holy Spirit convicts of judgment because the ruler of this world has been defeated by Your death, burial, and resurrection. You will use my proclamation of these truths to draw men, women, and children to Yourself in saving faith. That work of drawing people is the ministry of the Holy Spirit. Thank you, Father, for this assignment to be an imager and imitator of Jesus Christ.

John 16:12-15

12 "I have many more things to say to you, but you cannot
bear *them* at the present time. 13 But when He, the Spirit
of truth, comes, He will guide you into all the truth; for
He will not speak on His own, but whatever He hears, He
will speak; and He will disclose to you what is to
come. 14 He will glorify Me, for He will take from Mine
and will disclose *it* to you. 15 All things that the Father
has are Mine; this is why I said that He takes from Mine
and will disclose *it* to you.

Our Proclamation From John 16:12-15

Jesus, You tell me that when I trust in You for eternal life, I receive the Holy Spirit. You tell me that the Holy Spirit guides me into all truth because He will speak the words given to Him by You and Our Father. The words the Holy Spirit speaks will always glorify You and will always magnify what You have spoken because what You speak is the same thing that the Father speaks. These are the words the Holy Spirit will disclose to me.

Proverbs 4:1-9

1 Hear, O sons, the instruction of a father,
And give attention that you may gain understanding,
2 For I give you sound teaching;
Do not abandon my instruction.
3 When I was a son to my father,
Tender and the only son in the sight of my mother,
4 Then he taught me and said to me,
"Let your heart hold fast my words;
Keep my commandments and live;

Our Proclamation From Proverbs 4:1-9

Father, you desire that earthly fathers and mothers give themselves to instructing their children in your ways. Understanding is gained when I listen to Your instructions Father. You give me sound teaching and encourage me not to abandon Your instruction. When I was a son to my father and mother, You taught me to hold fast to Your words, to keep Your commandments that I might have life to the fullest.

This then is the path of inheriting wisdom, a path that can be passed down from generation to generation. Your instruction and the wisdom that accompanies it is the surest path to protecting, maintaining, and ensuring my family and all families that love You, are preserved through the years. May my children and grandchildren keep this chain unbroken so that they may enjoy Your goodness for as long as they live and until You return for us all.

James 1:12

12 Blessed is a man who perseveres under trial; for once he has been approved, he will receive the crown of life which *the Lord* has promised to those who love Him.

Our Proclamation From James 1:12

Lord, You say that I am blessed by persevering under trial, and that perseverance gains Your approval, and with it, a crown which signifies my love for You remains intact. I understand, Lord, that this means my perseverance is synonymous with my trust in You. I will persevere because my faith is real, it is genuine, and it is focused on You. Life is full of trials, and they will afflict me. I may suffer loss and look for all the world as if I have been defeated. But, when my trust in You remains through the storms of life, I have persevered in Your eyes, and you are well-pleased to proclaim my victory by giving to me the crown of life – the proof of my steadfast love for You and hope and faith in You.

James 1:13-15

13 Let no one say when he is tempted, “I am being
tempted by God”; for God cannot be tempted by evil, and
He Himself does not tempt anyone. 14 But each one is
tempted when he is carried away and enticed by his own
lust. 15 Then when lust has conceived, it gives birth to sin;
and when sin is accomplished, it brings forth death.

Our Proclamation From James 1:13-15

Father, I understand that all temptation comes from the devil or my own fleshy desires. You will never tempt me to sin. Therefore, when temptation comes to me, I must recognize it for what it is, and I must reject it immediately because it is inconsistent with Your nature. If I do not reject the temptation, I will begin to rationalize receiving the thing I am tempted by or toward. This is the “carrying away” process which hides the enflaming of my own lust. Enticement fuels lust and lust gives birth to sin. This happens when I allow my emotions or feelings to override my mind – what I know to do but do not do. Father, please keep me close to You and always warn me when I am straying from Your side.

Philippians 4:6-8

6 Be anxious for nothing, but in everything by prayer and
supplication with thanksgiving let your requests be made
known to God. 7 And the peace of God, which surpasses
all comprehension, will guard your hearts and your minds
in Christ Jesus.

8 Finally, brethren, whatever is true, whatever is
honorable, whatever is right, whatever is pure, whatever
is lovely, whatever is of good repute, if there is any
excellence and if anything worthy of praise, dwell on
these things.

Our Proclamation From Philippians 4:6-8

I am anxious for nothing, but in everything by prayer and supplication, with thanksgiving, I let my requests be made known to God. God's peace, which surpasses all understanding, will guard my heart and my mind in Christ Jesus.

I will meditate on, think deeply about, and practice those things that God shows me are true, honorable, right, pure, lovely, of good repute, are excellent and worthy of praise.

2 Kings 18:1-4

[1] Now it came about in the third year of Hoshea, the son
of Elah king of Israel, that Hezekiah the son of Ahaz king
of Judah became king. [2] He was twenty-five years old
when he became king, and he reigned twenty-nine years
in Jerusalem; and his mother's name was Abi the
daughter of Zechariah. [3] He did right in the sight of
the LORD, according to all that his father David had
done. [4] He removed the high places and broke down
the *sacred* pillars and cut down the Asherah. He also
broke in pieces the bronze serpent that Moses had made,
for until those days the sons of Israel burned incense to it;
and it was called Nehushtan.

Our Proclamation From 2 Kings 18:1-4

Father, you have shown me in Your Word that we all have choices to make concerning our walk with You. I cannot blame forever those who came before me. Hoshea, Elah, and Ahaz did evil in Your site. Amid generational evil, You raised up Hezekiah to lead Your people. Hezekiah did not follow in the footsteps of his lineage. I want to be like Hezekiah Lord. He honored You by destroying the "high places." Those high places are where people who have been deceived by idolatry, meet to further give their souls over to wickedness. Help me to hear Your Spirit speak so that I will not fall into deception. Help me to always see and destroy any sacred pillars in my life. Father, most importantly perhaps, help me to not see the vehicle used to bless me by Your promises, as something to be worshiped. I love You, the Giver of the promise, not the thing You might use to bless me. All the world's material things are merely "things of brass."

Ephesians 1:17-20

That the God of our Lord Jesus Christ, the Father of glory, may give to you a spirit of wisdom and of revelation in the knowledge of Him. I pray that the eyes of your heart may be enlightened, so that you will know what is the hope of His calling, what are the riches of the glory of His inheritance in the saints, and what is the surpassing greatness of His power toward us who believe. These are in accordance with the working of the strength of His might which He brought about in Christ, when He raised Him from the dead and seated Him at His right hand in the heavenly places. Ephesians 1:17-20

Our Proclamation From Ephesians 1:17-20

Thank you, Father, for giving me wisdom, revelation, and knowledge by and through Your Holy Spirit. Thank you for opening the eyes of my heart so that in this awakening I will understand the ministry of Jesus more fully and comprehend more fully who I am in Jesus – His inheritance! Thank you, Father, for helping me comprehend the surpassing greatness of the power that is at work in me – Your resurrection power, the same power that raised Jesus from the dead. I testify that Jesus is seated on His throne and highly exalted. I will honor Jesus in my life by seating Him on the throne of my life.

Isaiah 53:4-6

4 Surely our griefs He Himself bore,
And our sorrows He carried;
Yet we ourselves esteemed Him stricken,
Smitten of God, and afflicted.
5 But He was pierced through for our transgressions,
He was crushed for our iniquities;
The chastening for our well-being *fell* upon Him,
And by His scourging we are healed.
6 All of us like sheep have gone astray,
Each of us has turned to his own way;
But the LORD has caused the iniquity of us all
To fall on Him.

Our Proclamation From Isaiah 53:4-6

Father, what a great pronouncement of Your mercy and grace upon me You declare through Your prophet concerning Jesus the Christ, the eternal Son. You sent Him to bear my griefs, my sorrows, and indeed the griefs and sorrows of all people. This speaks of Jesus as my substitute, the One who bore my sins on Calvary's cross. Peter gave testimony to this truth when he wrote: "And He Himself bore our sins in His body on the cross, so that we might die to sin and live to righteousness; for by His wounds, you were healed" (1 Peter 2:24). It also speaks of Jesus as the perfect and spotless Lamb, who alone, is worthy and able to bear my sin. Finally, because Jesus bore my sin, He also bore the consequences of my sin – death. Therefore, I have life, eternal life through Jesus' sacrifice.

I am healed by Jesus' chastisement. This healing is in relation to the consequence of sin – death. So, I have been made sound, and well. The sacrifice of Jesus the Christ for me brought Yahweh's peace (meaning of "well-being"; see Strongs 7965e) upon me. This peace is received through faith in Jesus. It is spoken of as being reconciled to Yahweh (Rom. 5:10; 2 Cor. 5:18; Col. 1:22) by removing the basis of hostility (enmity – Eph. 2:15-16). Thus, my heavenly Father receives me because of Jesus' death and resurrection. The gift of eternal life is available to all who will believe.

Hebrews 10:11-14

[11] Every priest stands daily ministering and offering time
after time the same sacrifices, which can never take away
sins; [12] but He, having offered one sacrifice for sins for
all time, SAT DOWN AT THE RIGHT HAND OF
GOD, [13] waiting from that time onward UNTIL HIS
ENEMIES BE MADE A FOOTSTOOL FOR HIS FEET. [14] For by
one offering He has perfected for all time those who
are sanctified.

Our Proclamation From Hebrews 10:11-14

Father, you have saved me on the basis of faith, not on the basis of my works. Jesus offered Himself as a sacrifice for me, once for all time. That means I do not have to strive, work, or worry to maintain my salvation. Jesus has sat down at the place of honor, at the right hand of the Father, signifying that His atonement for me is complete because I have believed in Him. By Jesus' offering Himself, He has perfected me in my position as a son/daughter of God. Hallelujah!

Matthew 28:1-7

1 Now after the Sabbath, as it began to dawn toward the
first *day* of the week, Mary Magdalene and the other
Mary came to look at the grave. 2 And behold, a severe
earthquake had occurred, for an angel of the Lord
descended from heaven and came and rolled away the
stone and sat upon it. 3 And his appearance was like
lightning, and his clothing as white as snow. 4 The guards
shook for fear of him and became like dead men. 5 The
angel said to the women, "Do not be afraid; for I know
that you are looking for Jesus who has been
crucified. 6 He is not here, for He has risen, just as He
said. Come, see the place where He was lying. 7 Go
quickly and tell His disciples that He has risen from the
dead; and behold, He is going ahead of you into Galilee,
there you will see Him; behold, I have told you."

Our Proclamation From Matthew 28:1-7

On a Sunday morning, bright and clear, Mary Magdalene and Mary the wife of Clopas (John 19:25) came to the tomb where Jesus had been laid, expected to anoint His body. Upon their arrival a severe and very focused earthquake occurred which rolled away the stone blocking the entrance to the tomb. The source of that earthquake was an angel who descended from heaven and sat upon the stone that had been rolled away showing the opening to the place where it was supposed that Jesus laid. The guards passed out at the sight of the angel. The women were exhorted not to be fearful, but instead were told to remember what Jesus had told them previously. “He is not here, for He has risen, just as Her said,” was the exhortation that day. “Go and tell His disciples that He has risen from the dead.”

Our proclamation today and every day is the He has risen indeed. We serve a living Savior who will return one day soon. We will be ready for that day. In the meantime, we will be found faithful in telling the good news that Jesus saves!

Isaiah 61:1-3 KJV

The Spirit of the Lord GOD is upon me; because the LORD hath anointed me to preach good tidings unto the meek; he hath sent me to bind up the brokenhearted, to proclaim liberty to the captives, and the opening of the prison to them that are bound;

2 To proclaim the acceptable year of the LORD, and the day of vengeance of our God; to comfort all that mourn;

3 To appoint unto them that mourn in Zion, to give unto them beauty for ashes, the oil of joy for mourning, the garment of praise for the spirit of heaviness; that they might be called trees of righteousness, the planting of the LORD, that he might be glorified.

4 And they shall build the old wastes, they shall raise up the former desolations, and they shall repair the waste cities, the desolations of many generations.

Our Proclamation From Isaiah 61:1-3

The Holy Spirit of God lives in me. Yahweh has given me His anointing and therefore responsibility to tell people that Jesus saves! I must tell people that when Jesus saves, He brings healing to the broken hearted. I must tell all those trapped in the kingdom of darkness that they can be free and then teach them how those prison doors are opened. I must proclaim that today is the day of salvation for all who will believe in Jesus for eternal life. I must also tell people that Jesus is coming again to judge wickedness and set all things right. This message of salvation in Christ alone by faith alone brings joy to me and to all who mourn. The joy of the LORD is my garment of praise that replaces the spirit of heaviness that seeks to pull me away from Christ. In Christ I am firmly planted like a tree of righteousness to glorify Him.

2 Corinthians 5:17-19

[17] Therefore if anyone is in Christ, *he is* a new
creature; the old things passed away; behold, new things
have come. [18] Now all *these* things are from God, who
reconciled us to Himself through Christ and gave us
the ministry of reconciliation, [19] namely, that God was in
Christ reconciling the world to Himself, not counting
their trespasses against them, and He has committed to us
the word of reconciliation.

Our Proclamation From 2 Corinthians 5:17-19

Because I am saved, I abide in Christ. Abiding in Christ makes me a new creature. Who I was before Christ has passed away and I have become renewed. This new life I now live, I live because God loves me. It was God's love for me that reconciled me to Him through my faith in Christ's death on my behalf. God desires that I serve Him by telling others about Jesus and by doing that I am serving Him in a ministry of reconciliation.

John 14:1-6

[1] "Do not let your heart be troubled; believe in God,
believe also in Me. [2] In My Father's house are many
dwelling places; if it were not so, I would have told you;
for I go to prepare a place for you. [3] If I go and prepare a
place for you, I will come again and receive you to
Myself, that where I am, *there* you may be also. [4] And
you know the way where I am going." [5] Thomas said to
Him, "Lord, we do not know where You are going, how
do we know the way?" [6] Jesus said to him, "I am the way,
and the truth, and the life; no one comes to the Father but
through Me.

Our Proclamation From John 14:1-6

Jesus, You have exhorted me to not become troubled, to hold fast to my faith in Yahweh and You. You have described my eternal home as a mansion my Father owns which has a place You have built for me. You have promised me that where You are, I will one day be as well. You are the way to eternal life. You are the one true way to eternal life. No one will receive eternal life unless and until they have trusted in Your finished work on their behalf. There is no other way to the Father but through faith in You.

Ephesians 2:1-10

1 And you were dead in your trespasses and sins, 2 in
which you formerly walked according to the course
of this world, according to the prince of the power of the
air, of the spirit that is now working in the sons of
disobedience. 3 Among them we too all formerly lived
in the lusts of our flesh, indulging the desires of the flesh
and of the mind, and were by nature children of
wrath, even as the rest. 4 But God, being rich in mercy,
because of His great love with which He loved us, 5 even
when we were dead in our transgressions, made us alive
together with Christ (by grace you have been
saved), 6 and raised us up with Him, and seated us with
Him in the heavenly *places* in Christ Jesus, 7 so that in
the ages to come He might show the surpassing riches of
His grace in kindness toward us in Christ Jesus. 8 For by
grace you have been saved through faith; and that not of
yourselves, *it is* the gift of God; 9 not as a result of works,
so that no one may boast. 10 For we are His
workmanship, created in Christ Jesus for good works,
which God prepared beforehand so that we would walk
in them.

Our Proclamation From Ephesians 2:1-10

I was spiritually dead in my trespasses and sins. My life was lived just like every other person who had no faith in God. My life was ruled by the lusts of my flesh, and I indulged in the things I desired and on which my mind focused. Because of that God's judgment abided upon me. But God's mercy and love for me reached down and even when I was dead spiritually, He made me alive by His grace through faith in Jesus. My inheritance and destiny are now heaven. My testimony to God's goodness tells everyone that God is rich in mercy and kindness. I am His workmanship created by faith in Christ Jesus for the purpose of doing the things God assigns me to do In this life.

Job 12:24-25

24 "He deprives of intelligence the chiefs of the earth's
people
And makes them wander in a pathless waste.
25 "They grope in darkness with no light,
And He makes them stagger like a drunken man.

Our Proclamation From Job 12:24-25

Father, the headlines of our times are a constant drumbeat of arrogant self-autonomy, declaring each individual's right to create their own world and reality. Supporting this madness are the governments of the world, the state-sponsored and controlled media, and every educational institution that depends on governments for their financial existence. On a global scale, individuals and their not-so-secret organizations are revealing their long-hidden plans to consolidate their power and control over every aspect of Your creation, subjecting people to their vision of the future.

Yet, I will not fear, nor will I succumb to dismay or despair because I know Who rules the affairs of man. In their striving to become gods they have forgotten You and Your eternal declaration that it is the fool who says in his/her heart there is no GOD. You, father, have looked on while the evildoers in our midst have declared their own brilliance and victory, yet You have displaced true intelligence, which is acknowledging and serving You, and allowed those who reject You to wander on pathless wastelands. Thinking themselves wise they have become fools. They grope in darkness without the Light; they stagger like a drunken man. Such is the destiny of all who refuse Your loving call to reconciliation through faith in the Lord Jesus Christ.

1 Corinthians 8:4-6

4 Therefore concerning the eating of things sacrificed to
idols, we know that there is no such thing as an idol in
the world, and that there is no God but one. 5 For even
if there are so-called gods whether in heaven or on earth,
as indeed there are many gods and many lords, 6 yet for
us there is *but* one God, the Father, from whom are all
things and we *exist* for Him; and one Lord, Jesus
Christ, by whom are all things, and we *exist* through
Him.

Explanation and Proclamation From 1 Corinthians 8:4-6

Here is the Greek - ἀλλ' ἡμῖν εἷς θεὸς ὁ πατήρ, ἐξ οὗ τὰ πάντα καὶ ἡμεῖς εἰς αὐτόν, καὶ εἷς κύριος Ἰησοῦς Χριστός, δι' οὗ τὰ πάντα καὶ ἡμεῖς δι' αὐτοῦ.

Explanation - the word κύριος (kyrios) is used consistently in the NT to translate the OT tetragrammaton, YHWH. And since the OT consistently declared that YHWH was God (1 Kings 8:60, 18:39, Josh. 22:34, Deut. 4:39, Ps. 100:3, 118:27, 2 Chron. 33;13, Isa. 45:18), 1 Cor. 8:6 is also saying that Jesus is Jehovah God as well. Note further, that Jesus in Isa. 9:6 is also called "Mighty God, Everlasting Father".

John 10:30 – "I and the Father are one." John 8:58 – "Before Abraham was, I am." Jesus is Yahweh incarnate – Revelation 1:8, 22:13 – the "Alpha and Omega." The point – Jesus is God. He is the divine second person of the three person Trinity. Three persons, one essence.

Philippians 3:7-8

[7] But whatever things were gain to me, those things I
have counted as loss for the sake of Christ. [8] More than
that, I count all things to be loss in view of the surpassing value of knowing Christ Jesus my Lord, for whom I have suffered the loss of all things, and count them but rubbish so that I may gain Christ…

Our Proclamation From Philippians 3:7-8

Both my "secular and spiritual resumes" – those things that I have achieved in life and that I once believed were significant and held up before a watching world to claim my relevance, importance, and identity have all now paled in comparison to knowing my Lord Jesus Christ (things such as nationality, ethnicity; spiritual markers such as denomination, baptism, church membership; righteousness, holiness, and zealousness based on my own actions). Further, I willingly give up all those earthly identities to be known now as a son/daughter of Yahweh through faith in Yeshua. The difference between the value of the things of this world and of knowing Jesus Christ as Lord is immeasurable. Therefore, all that the world holds dear, that I myself once held dear, are seen as rubbish when compared to gaining eternal life through Jesus Christ.

Philippians 3:8-11

8 More than that, I count all things to be loss in view of
the surpassing value of knowing Christ Jesus my
Lord, for whom I have suffered the loss of all things, and
count them but rubbish so that I may gain Christ, 9 and
may be found in Him, not having a righteousness of my
own derived from *the* Law, but that which is through
faith in Christ, the righteousness which *comes* from God
on the basis of faith, 10 that I may know Him and the
power of His resurrection and the fellowship of His
sufferings, being conformed to His death; 11 in order that
I may attain to the resurrection from the dead.

Our Proclamation From Philippians 3:8-11

Nothing the world can offer me is worthy to be compared with my identity and standing in faith in Jesus Christ. The righteousness that I have is Christ's, and it has been given to me not on the basis of my works, good behavior, or worthiness, but only because by faith I have trusted in Jesus for eternal life. This spiritual transformation has been wrought in me by the same power that raised Jesus from the dead. Therefore, I desire to know Him more fully including His sufferings on my behalf, so that in my own sufferings He is found a faithful companion in my weakness. I longingly look forward to my own resurrection when I will come out from among the dead to be eternally in His presence.

Proverbs 31:10-12, 26, 28-30

10 An excellent wife, who can find?
For her worth is far above jewels.
11 The heart of her husband trusts in her,
And he will have no lack of gain.
12 She does him good and not evil
All the days of her life.

26 She opens her mouth in wisdom,
And the teaching of kindness is on her tongue.
28 Her children rise up and bless her;
Her husband *also*, and he praises her, *saying*:
29 "Many daughters have done nobly,
But you excel them all."
30 Charm is deceitful and beauty is vain,
But a woman who fears the LORD, she shall be praised.

Our Proclamation From Proverbs 31

Father, You instruct men in Proverbs 31 to diligently seek a wife who loves and honors You. The woman who loves you is priceless in Your eyes and must be in mine also. When I know that my wife loves You above all else, I will trust her with my heart. Together, a man and woman who seek the Lord together will receive great spiritual gain, worth far more than the world's riches. A wife who trusts You implicitly, will seek my good always. Together we become a steady and sure testimony to what marriage was designed to be. I must seek a wife who is wise in Your ways, who speaks kindness. This wife and mother will be praised by her husband and children, for they see in her an exceedingly noble and righteous woman who loves and fears the Lord first and foremost.

2 Peter 3:9-13

9 The Lord is not slow about His promise, as some count
slowness, but is patient toward you, not wishing for any
to perish but for all to come to repentance.

10 But the day of the Lord will come like a thief, in
which the heavens will pass away with a roar and
the elements will be destroyed with intense heat, and the
earth and its works will be burned up.

11 Since all these things are to be destroyed in this way,
what sort of people ought you to be in holy conduct and
godliness, 12 looking for and hastening the coming of the
day of God, because of which the heavens will be
destroyed by burning, and the elements will melt with
intense heat! 13 But according to His promise we are
looking for new heavens and a new earth, in which
righteousness dwells.

Our Proclamation From 2 Peter 3:9-13

Father you are faithful and true. You will fulfill Your promises in Your own time. Because of Your patience and Your desire that none would perish, You lead many to faith. You will send Jesus at the appointed time to receive to Himself His bride, the ecclesia. When Your day comes, what we call "the day of the Lord," will come with devastation; the heavens will pass away with a roar as will the earth and all material things. Because I understand this truth from Your holy Scriptures, I must be holy in my conduct, with all godliness in every way, eagerly awaiting that day when you will set all things right according to Your wisdom and promise.

John 3:14-18

[14] As Moses lifted up the serpent in the wilderness, even
so must the Son of Man be lifted up; [15] so that
whoever believes will in Him have eternal life.

[16] "For God so loved the world, that He gave His only
begotten Son, that whoever believes in Him shall not
perish, but have eternal life. [17] For God did not send the
Son into the world to judge the world, but that the world
might be saved through Him. [18] He who believes in Him
is not judged; he who does not believe has been judged
already, because he has not believed in the name
of the only begotten Son of God.

Our Proclamation From John 3:14-18

Father, You have informed me in Your Word that salvation is by faith alone. Whoever believes the testimony of Jesus, that He came to seek and to save that which was lost; that He gave His life in full payment of the debt of sin I owed which was death; and that He rose from the dead, appearing to hundreds before He ascended back to the glory He had before He came to this earth. This was and always will remain the supreme example of Your love for me – Jesus Christ. Jesus came to this earth the first time not to judge it, but to offer Himself for salvation to all who will believe. Those who believe inherit eternal life and escape the coming judgment at the time of the end. Rejection of Jesus in this life is a self-proclaimed judgment in eternity.

Galatians 6:1-2

[1] Brethren, even if anyone is caught in any trespass, you
who are spiritual, restore such a one in a spirit of
gentleness; *each one* looking to yourself, so that you too
will not be tempted. [2] Bear one another's burdens, and
thereby fulfill the law of Christ.

Our Proclamation From Galatians 6:1-2

Brothers and sisters, it is our responsibility to assist other believers when they stumble into sin. Their stumbling may be at the end of a long chain of sinful behavior, or it may be the result of being blindsided by sin that they did not know they were walking into. Those of us who are "spiritual" which means walking in faith and right relationship with Jesus must come alongside of fallen believers and help them stand up again. We may have to hold them up for they will be weakened by their sin. We are to hold an attitude of gentleness and lovingkindness, remembering our own weakness and the power of grace that surely restores (Greek – *kataritzo* – to mend or repair; to make useful again). This then fulfills the law of Christ which is to love one another as He commanded us to do in order to fulfill the law (Romans 13:8; Galatians 5:14).

Galatians 5:1-4

1 It was for freedom that Christ set us free; therefore keep standing firm and do not be subject again to a yoke of slavery.

2 Behold I, Paul, say to you that if you
receive circumcision, Christ will be of no benefit to
you. 3 And I testify again to every man who
receives circumcision, that he is under obligation to keep
the whole Law. 4 You have been severed from Christ, you
who are seeking to be justified by law; you have fallen
from grace.

Our Proclamation From Galatians 5:1-4

Father, You have freed me from wrong thinking concerning salvation. You freely gave me Your gift of salvation through faith in Jesus Christ. The law could not bring about my reconciliation to You. The requirements of Your law were fulfilled in Jesus and therefore I now live by the law of Christ and by the power of the Spirit. In Christ alone and in His love for me I stand.

I can never be perfected by works of the flesh no matter how fervently I practice them. Church membership, attendance, baptism, giving financially, feeding the homeless, caring for the poor, and every other thing I might do cannot save me. If I am trying to be found righteous by those actions, then I have severed myself from Christ and He has become of no benefit to me. The grace of Yahweh is all sufficient for me. In Christ I find my complete and total rest, comfort, and salvation.

2 Thessalonians 2:1-8

1 Now we request you, brethren, with regard to
the coming of our Lord Jesus Christ and our gathering
together to Him, 2 that you not be quickly shaken from
your composure or be disturbed either by a spirit or
a message or a letter as if from us, to the effect that the
day of the Lord has come. 3 Let no one in any way
deceive you, for *it will not come* unless the apostasy
comes first, and the man of lawlessness is revealed,
the son of destruction, 4 who opposes and exalts himself
above every so-called god or object of worship, so that he
takes his seat in the temple of God, displaying himself as
being God. 5 Do you not remember that while I was still
with you, I was telling you these things? 6 And you
know what restrains him now, so that in his time he will
be revealed. 7 For the mystery of lawlessness is already at
work; only he who now restrains *will do so* until he is
taken out of the way. 8 Then that lawless one will be
revealed whom the Lord will slay with the breath of His
mouth and bring to an end by the appearance of
His coming.

Our Proclamation From 2 Thessalonians 2:1-8

Father, Your Word tells us that Jesus is coming again for His ecclesia. We will not be shaken by skeptics and doubters who say there is no rapture. The return of Jesus for His body will happen BEFORE the eschatological

"Day of the LORD." Before the Day of the LORD but after the rapture of the ecclesia, the man of lawlessness will be revealed, the one the Scriptures call the Antichrist. When the Antichrist arrives, he will seek to be worshipped as Yahweh. In order to do that, the lawless one will set himself up as god in the reconstructed temple of the Tribulation period. None of this can happen until the Restrainer is removed. The Restrainer and those the Restrainer reside in, the body of Christ, will be removed simultaneously.

1 Thessalonians 4:13-18

13 But we do not want you to be uninformed, brethren,
about those who are asleep, so that you will not grieve as
do the rest who have no hope. 14 For if we believe that
Jesus died and rose again, even so God will bring with
Him those who have fallen asleep in Jesus. 15 For this we
say to you by the word of the Lord, that we who are
alive and remain until the coming of the Lord, will not
precede those who have fallen asleep. 16 For the
Lord Himself will descend from heaven with a shout,
with the voice of *the* archangel and with the trumpet of
God, and the dead in Christ will rise first. 17 Then we who
are alive and remain will be caught up together with
them in the clouds to meet the Lord in the air, and so we
shall always be with the Lord. 18 Therefore comfort one
another with these words.

Our Proclamation From 1 Thessalonians 4:13-18

Christians should not be uninformed about the rapture of the ecclesia, especially those who have died loving Jesus Christ. We believe that Jesus rose from the grave, a type of first fruits to Yahweh (1 Cor. 15:20). Jesus' resurrection proves our own resurrection/rapture to Him. "God will bring with Him" means those who died before the rapture will rise first and be joined by those who are alive when the rapture occurs, to join Jesus in the air and ascend to heaven's dimension. The rapture is a primary doctrine of our faith and deserves much more attention than it currently does. We are exhorted to "comfort one another with these words." It is not comforting to disparage or deny the rapture.

Matthew 28:16-20

16 But the eleven disciples proceeded to Galilee, to the mountain which Jesus had designated. 17 When they saw Him, they worshiped *Him*; but some were doubtful. 18 And Jesus came up and spoke to them, saying, "All authority has been given to Me in heaven and on earth. 19 Go therefore and make disciples of all the nations, baptizing them in the name of the Father and the Son and the Holy Spirit, 20 teaching them to observe all that I commanded you; and lo, I am with you always, even to the end of the age."

Our Proclamation From Matthew 28:16-20

Father, help me to comprehend what it means to be a child of Yours. Help me to grasp what my responsibilities are as Your son/daughter. Help me to never forget that Jesus has all authority in Your creation (in heaven and on earth), and He has delegated that to me. Therefore, I have the power of the Holy Spirit living within me and enabling me to achieve all that You assign to me. You have told me specifically that I am responsible to make disciples from among all the people groups of the earth (all the nations). You have commanded me to baptize them in Your name Father, in the name of Jesus our Lord and Savior, and in the name of the Holy Spirit who empowers us. After baptism, all men and women are to be discipled, which means that they are to be taught to observe (obey) all that You have commanded through Your Word, the Bible. You have promised never to leave me and so I will serve You faithfully in this great commission to teach everyone Your Word for Your honor and Glory.

Romans 13:8-10

[8] Owe nothing to anyone except to love one another;
for he who loves his neighbor has fulfilled *the* law. [9] For
this, "YOU SHALL NOT COMMIT ADULTERY, YOU SHALL NOT MURDER, YOU SHALL NOT STEAL, YOU SHALL NOT COVET," and if there is any other commandment, it is summed up in this saying, "YOU SHALL LOVE YOUR NEIGHBOR AS YOURSELF." [10] Love does no wrong to a
neighbor; therefore love is the fulfillment of *the* law.

Our Proclamation From Romans 8:8-10

Father, you have commanded Your people to love one another and to love our enemies. You have taught us to bless those who persecute us (Rom. 12:14), to never pay back evil for evil to anyone (Rom. 12:17), to never take our own revenge (Rom. 12:19), to care for the needs of our enemy (Rom. 12:20), to never allow our love the freedom to take advantage of others (Gal. 5:13), to never rejoice in things that are false or unrighteous (1 Cor. 13:6), to never deliberately cause another to stumble morally or spiritually (Rom. 14:21), and, "Above all, keep fervent in your love for one another, because love covers a multitude of sins" (1 Peter 4:8).

Instead, we are to love one another as a testimony to the world.

- By this all men will know that you are My disciples, if you have love for one another (John 13:35).
- Serving Christ means serving other people (Matt. 25:35-36).
- Serving other people demonstrates our love for You Father (Heb. 6:10).
- The one who loves his brother abides in the light (1 John 2:10).
- Beloved, let us love one another for love is from God; and everyone who loves is born of God and knows God (1 John 4:7).

Paul's point in this passage from Romans is that when Christian's love as the Scriptures command us to love we are fulfilling the moral requirements of the Law and therefore do no wrong to our neighbor, but instead, will love them through our actions as we love ourselves through our actions.

Romans 13:11-14

[11] *Do* this (my note – love), knowing the time, that it
is already the hour for you to awaken from sleep; for
now salvation is nearer to us than when we
believed. [12] The night is almost gone, and the day is near.
Therefore let us lay aside the deeds of darkness and put
on the armor of light. [13] Let us behave properly as in the
day, not in carousing and drunkenness, not in sexual
promiscuity and sensuality, not in strife and
jealousy. [14] But put on the Lord Jesus Christ, and make
no provision for the flesh in regard to *its* lusts.

Our Proclamation From Romans 13:11-14

Loving Yahweh and loving our neighbor keeps me in tune, living in the same frequency with my Creator. This in turn enables me to comprehend the hour in which I live biblically. The hour is late, and Jesus is returning soon, therefore I must not be distracted or confused by the things I see or hear which emanate from Babylon. This present darkness is almost gone and the coming of the Son of Man will bring a new day. Therefore, I will discipline myself and ask the Holy Spirit to enable me to lay aside all deeds of darkness, making no allowance for my fleshly and carnal lusts that wage war against me. Instead, I will put on the armor of Light and be His imager so that when the flesh rises up, I will put it down by the power of the Lord Jesus Christ in me.

Acts 20:22-24

[22] And now, behold, bound by the Spirit, I am on my way to Jerusalem, not knowing what will happen to me there, [23] except that the Holy Spirit solemnly testifies to me in every city, saying that bonds and afflictions await me. [24] But I do not consider my life of any account as dear to myself, so that I may finish my course and the ministry which I received from the Lord Jesus, to testify solemnly of the gospel of the grace of God.

Our Proclamation From Acts 20:22-24

Father, I understand that Your Holy Spirit will lead me everywhere You have directed Him to lead me. There may be instances when under the Holy Spirit's leading, I'll be led to go someplace where difficult times may transpire. Your Spirit may lead me to have difficult discussions with people. My life is Yours Father. I do not consider my life to be set apart for me, but for Your glory. I only know this LORD, my life is in Your hands, and my desire is to finish my course and the ministry I have received from my Lord Jesus. As part of this finishing the course, I will constantly point people to You and will solemnly testify to Your grace.

Proverbs 16:1-3

[1] The plans of the heart belong to man,
But the answer of the tongue is from the LORD.
[2] All the ways of a man are clean in his own sight,
But the LORD weighs the motives.
[3] Commit your works to the LORD
And your plans will be established.

Our Proclamation From Proverbs 16:1-3

Father, You have created me to be a reasoning, thinking, intelligent man/woman. You have encouraged me to seek You and the wisdom You give to all who ask it of You. While I may develop my plans based on my thoughts, emotions, and will, when I am abiding in You, I will receive from You the words, answers, righteous responses needed in every situation. In my own sight I often believe my motives are pure. I am thankful that You correct me when my motivations for things are not of You. I will commit myself to Your ways Father so that my thoughts are Your thoughts and therefore my plans are the plans You desire for me.

Psalm 55:22-23

22 Cast your burden upon the LORD and He will sustain
you; He will never allow the righteous to be shaken.
23 But You, O God, will bring them down to the pit of
destruction; Men of bloodshed and deceit will not live
out half their days. But I will trust in You.

Our Proclamation From Psalm 55:22-23

I will cast my burden upon You, LORD, because You have promised to sustain me. Whatever my burden looks like, when I come to You and lay it at Your feet, You will sustain me. As I keep my focus upon You, you will not allow me to be shaken such that I would ever lose my faith. Those who seek to oppress me and shake my faith by their words or actions will face You one day. By their actions they shorten their own life. You take them down to the pit of destruction. Regardless of what comes my way I will trust in You.

Ephesians 5:6-8

6 Let no one deceive you with empty words, for because
of these things the wrath of God comes upon the sons of
disobedience. 7 Therefore do not be partakers with
them; 8 for you were formerly darkness, but now you are
Light in the Lord; walk as children of Light.

Our Proclamation From Ephesians 5:6-8

Father, I will not allow anyone to deceive me with empty words. Empty words are those things spoken that are devoid of Your Holy Spirit. Empty words are those things that Your Holy Spirit opposes. In order to not be deceived by empty words I must learn to hear Your voice and to respond to You and to the things You say to me which are life. Your wrath will one day fall upon all those who speak empty words for they are sons of disobedience. I will honor You and not become partakers in the works of disobedience. I am able to walk in the Light, which is Jesus, because You have delivered me from the kingdom of darkness. Thank you, Father, for enabling me to walk as Your child in the Light.

Psalm 34:1-3

[1] I will bless the LORD at all times;
His praise shall continually be in my mouth.
[2] My soul will make its boast in the LORD;
The humble will hear it and rejoice.
[3] O magnify the LORD with me,
And let us exalt His name together.

Our Proclamation From Psalm 34:1-3

Because of your steadfast love for me Father, I will bless your name at all times. I would have no desire to bless Your name without You first having touched my life. I will not allow the enemy to deceive me and cause me to doubt Your goodness for me. It means I will not attribute evil to You, nor believe a false report from anyone who denigrates Your name. Praise for You shall continually be on my lips.

When I do boast it will be in You, in Your goodness, mercy, and grace. Those whom You have been calling, the humble, they will hear my words as a testimony to Your goodness and I trust You will draw them to Yourself through faith in Jesus. I encourage all my family and friends to magnify the LORD with me today and every day. Especially when we come together as the body of Christ, may we all exalt His name together.

Psalm 34:4-7

4 I sought the LORD, and He answered me,
And delivered me from all my fears.
5 They looked to Him and were radiant,
And their faces will never be ashamed.
6 This poor man cried, and the LORD heard him
And saved him out of all his troubles.
7 The angel of the LORD encamps around those who fear Him,
And rescues them.

Our Proclamation From Psalm 34:4-7

Fear, worry, and/or anxiety need not be carried as a burden. I have a Father in heaven who hears my every cry and desires to lift every burden from my heart and mind. He will deliver me when I seek Him in prayer. In fact, all those who look to Yahweh for deliverance will be blessed and never ashamed for trusting Him. I will not trust in earthly things to secure my deliverance, nor my own plans or knowledge. I am poor in the eyes of the world because I trust in Yahweh not material things. The truth is I am rich because He watches over me. Yahweh will protect and rescue His people who rightly worship and fear Him.

Psalm 63:1-4

1 O God, You are my God; I shall seek You earnestly;
My soul thirsts for You, my flesh yearns for You,
In a dry and weary land where there is no water.
2 Thus I have seen You in the sanctuary,
To see Your power and Your glory.
3 Because Your lovingkindness is better than life,
My lips will praise You.
4 So I will bless You as long as I live;
I will lift up my hands in Your name.

Our Proclamation From Psalm 63:1-4

Yahweh, You are my God. I shall earnestly seek You. My soul thirsts, my flesh yearns for what only You can provide – satisfaction to my soul, spiritual food for my spirit, the refreshing relief of Your presence as is the cool water that revitalizes my weariness. In Your Word I behold You in Your sanctuary (Isaiah 6; Ezekiel 1; Revelation 4). I am witness to Your power and glory in all of creation and in every relationship and individual I see through Your eyes. Because receiving Your lovingkindness is better than anything else I might receive in life, I praise you. I will constantly bless Your name with my lips as long as I live, and I will lift up my hands in worship as a testimony to our goodness.

Isaiah 55:1-3

1 Ho! Everyone who thirsts, come to the waters;
And you who have no money come, buy and eat.
Come, buy wine and milk
Without money and without cost.
2 "Why do you spend money for what is not bread,
And your wages for what does not satisfy?
Listen carefully to Me, and eat what is good,
And delight yourself in abundance.
3 "Incline your ear and come to Me.
Listen, that you may live;
And I will make an everlasting covenant with you,
According to the faithful mercies shown to David.

Our Proclamation From Isaiah 55:1-3

Father, You are righteous and holy. You have issued a proclamation to all your creation to come to You and receive living water. All who thirst are welcome to come to You and You will not impede any who come. You offer me eternal salvation without cost to me, for I have no money that could possibly purchase my redemption. You have counseled Your creation to not waste time, energy, or wealth trying to acquire the things of this world which cannot not by design satisfy me in any meaningful way. I will listen to You carefully; I will incline my ear to You so that I may receive the Word from Your mouth which is given in abundance to me freely. You have promised me an everlasting covenant according to Your faithful mercies shown to me in Jesus Christ.

1 Corinthians 2:9-11

9 but just as it is written,

"THINGS WHICH EYE HAS NOT SEEN AND EAR HAS NOT HEARD,
AND *which* HAVE NOT ENTERED THE HEART OF MAN,
ALL THAT GOD HAS PREPARED FOR THOSE WHO LOVE HIM."

10 For to us God revealed *them* through the Spirit; for the
Spirit searches all things, even the depths of God.
11 For
who among men knows the *thoughts* of a man except the spirit of the man which is in him? Even so the *thoughts* of God no one knows except the Spirit of God.

Our Proclamation From 1 Corinthians 2:9-11

Father, You are much more than I can describe or explain. You have things You desire to do that no eye has yet seen, nor ear has yet heard. These things are so high and lofty that they have not even entered into my heart. What You have decided on behalf of those who love You is beyond beautiful and marvelous, and I believe will leave me humbled and speechless when at last I finally behold them.

Your Holy Spirit reveals to those who love You all the things necessary to wait upon You, to serve You in honor and righteousness, to learn and grow in faith, and to love Your sons and daughters, even if different from us. Help me Father to trust in You in all things and keep me focused on my Lord and Savior Jesus the Christ.

Luke 2:1-14

1 Now in those days a decree went out from Caesar Augustus, that a census be taken of all the inhabited earth. 2 This was the first census taken while Quirinius was governor of Syria. 3 And everyone was on his way to register for the census, each to his own city. 4 Joseph also went up from Galilee, from the city of Nazareth, to Judea, to the city of David which is called Bethlehem, because he was of the house and family of David, 5 in order to register along with Mary, who was engaged to him, and was with child. 6 While they were there, the days were completed for her to give birth. 7 And she gave birth to her firstborn son; and she wrapped Him in cloths, and laid Him in a manger, because there was no room for them in the inn.

8 In the same region there were *some* shepherds staying out in the fields and keeping watch over their flock by night. 9 And an angel of the Lord suddenly stood before them, and the glory of the Lord shone around them; and they were terribly frightened. 10 But the angel said to them, "Do not be afraid; for behold, I bring you good news of great joy which will be for all the people; 11 for today in the city of David there has been born for you a Savior, who is Christ the Lord. 12 This *will be* a sign for you: you will find a baby wrapped in cloths and lying in a manger." 13 And suddenly there appeared with the angel a multitude of the heavenly host praising God and saying,

14 "Glory to God in the highest,
And on earth peace among men with whom He is pleased."

Our Proclamation From Luke 2:1-14

Father, I know now that real life begins when people understand that You have made a way for all of Your creatures, every man and woman ever born, to be reconciled to You. That reconciliation is made possible because of Jesus, Who gave His life for us all. Therefore, whosoever believes in Him shall not perish but has everlasting life from the moment they believe. May that truth be on my lips everyday of life You give me so that everyone You provide a divine encounter with, has the opportunity to make this life and eternity changing choice clearly expressed to them. All glory and honor belong to our great God.

ABOUT THE AUTHOR

Mike Spaulding was ordained to the ministry in 1998. Since then, he has planted two Calvary Chapel churches - Calvary Christian Fellowship, St. Marys, Ohio, in 1998, and Calvary Chapel of Lima, Ohio, in 2005, where he currently serves as pastor.

Mike holds a B.A. in Organizational Management from Bluffton University, an M.T.S. from Logos Graduate School, and a Ph.D. in apologetics from Trinity College of the Bible and Theological Seminary.

Mike is the host of Soaring Eagle Radio (www.soaringeagleradio.com) and cohosts The Kingdom War Room with Dr. Michael Lake (www.kingdomintelligencebriefing.com), and The SPOTT Report with his wife Kathy (www.drmikespaulding.com).

His teaching ministry is featured on the radio program "The Transforming Word," heard on radio stations throughout the Midwest United States.

Mike has been married to his lovely wife Kathy for over 41 years and together they have four daughters, seven grandchildren, and two great-grandchildren.

You may contact Mike via email – drmichaelspaulding@gmail.com or by writing him at the address below.
Send your gifts to support this ministry to:

Dr. Mike Spaulding
P.O. Box 3007
Elida, Ohio 45807

You may donate online to The Transforming Word Ministries by:

Swipe Simple (Preferred) Transforming Word Global Ecclesia Ministries
https://swipesimple.com/links/lnk_661b3836

Venmo – @TWGEM

Cash App - $TransformingWordGEM

PayPal – support@drmikespaulding.com

The Transforming Word Publishing is a ministry of the House of Spaulding, an ecclesiastical ministry not associated with any governmental entity or oversight.

OTHER BOOKS BY MIKE SPAULDING

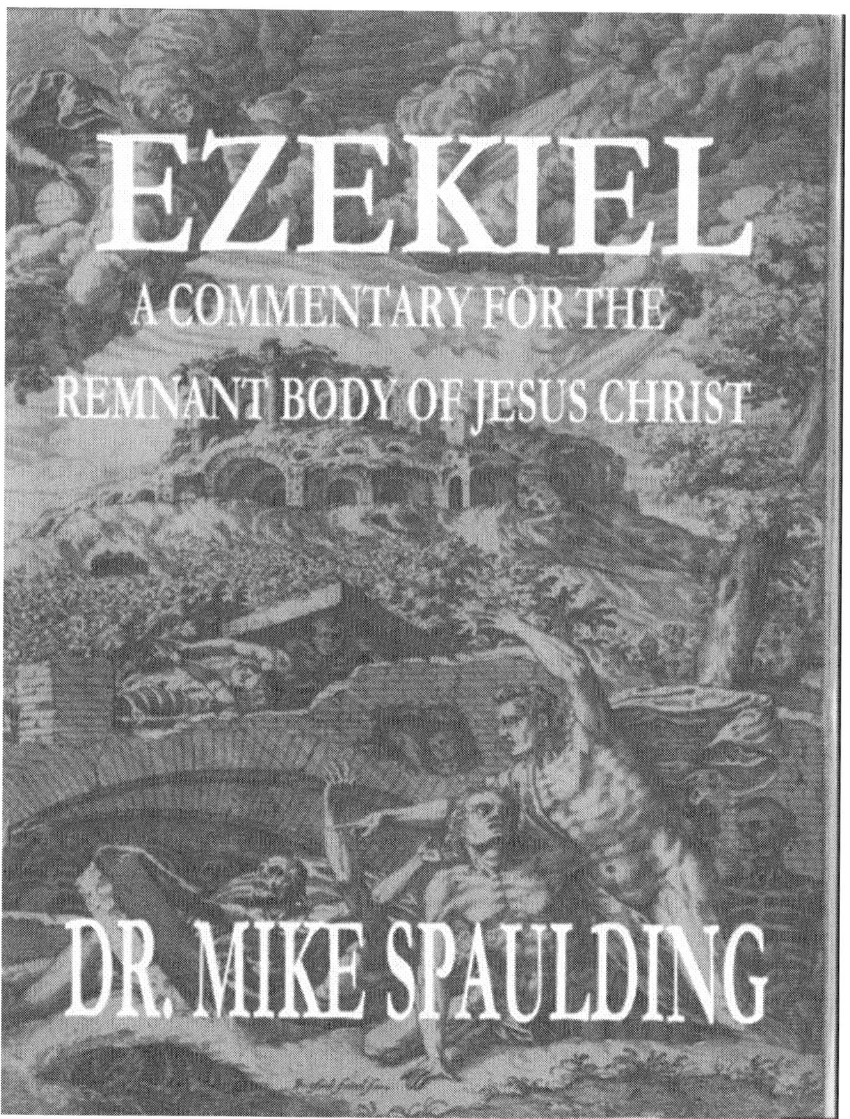

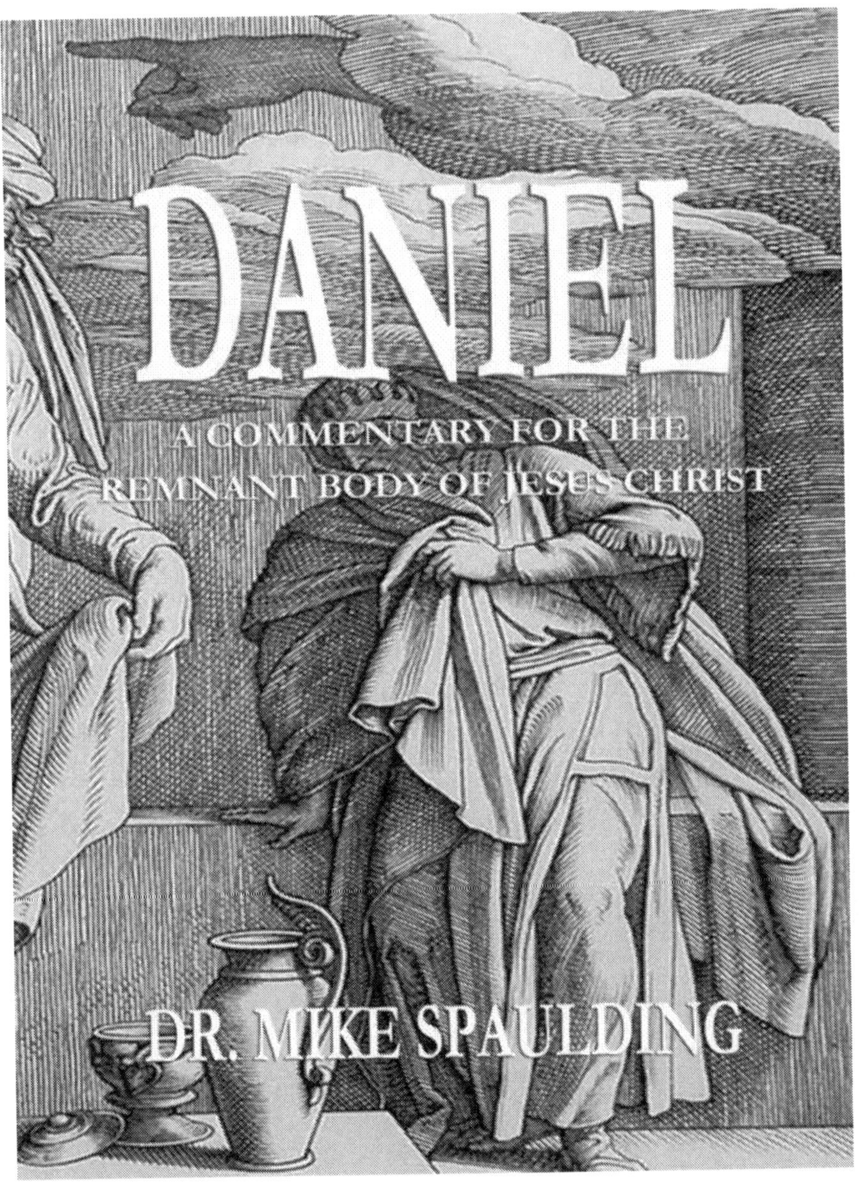
DANIEL
A COMMENTARY FOR THE
REMNANT BODY OF JESUS CHRIST
DR. MIKE SPAULDING

THE GOSPEL OF
MARK
A COMMENTARY FOR THE
REMNANT BODY OF JESUS CHRIST
STUDY GUIDE INCLUDED
DR. MIKE SPAULDING

THE REVELATION OF JESUS CHRIST TO JOHN

A COMMENTARY FOR THE REMNANT BODY OF JESUS CHRIST

DR. MIKE SPAULDING

THE FOUR HORSES
OF REVELATION 6
A NEW PROPHETIC INTERPRETATION
DR. MIKE SPAULDING

DANIEL'S
SEVENTY
WEEKS
A COMMENTARY ON DANIEL 9
DR. MIKE
SPAULDING

Dr. Mike Spaulding
LETTERS FROM
Jesus
What the seven Ecclesias
of Revelation 2-3 say to us today
2321
foreword by
Pastor Caspar McCloud
Letters from Jesus | What the Seven Ecclesias of Revelation 2-3 Say to Us Today | Dr. Mike Spaulding
WORD

JAMES

A COMMENTARY FOR THE
REMNANT BODY OF JESUS CHRIST

DR. MIKE SPAULDING

1 CORINTHIANS

A COMMENTARY FOR THE
REMNANT BODY OF JESUS CHRIST

DR. MIKE SPAULDING

UPSIDEDOWN
IN
AMERICA
What went wrong and how do we make it right again?
AT CHURCH
AT HOME
WITH OUR LEADERS
FOREWORD BY
DR. MICHAEL
LAKE
MIKE SPAULDING

Made in the USA
Columbia, SC
16 November 2024

46579457R00100